WHAT THOSE
E.

MW01102699

'The title says it all. *Extraordinary You* is filled with gems of inner wisdom and inspiring stories from eleven great leaders that will expand your mind and help you truly live a more vibrant, authentic and extraordinary life.'

~ **DR. JOHN F. DEMARTINI**
Founder of the Demartini Institute, Author of *The Breakthrough Experience -
A Revolutionary New Approach to Personal Transformation*

'*Extraordinary You* is a must-read that inspires the human spirit to new heights. Thanks to these eleven amazing authors, I will never say "I'm bored" again, but rather, I will live life full out and end up fully spent and joyous!'

~ **DONNA DAISY, PH.D.**
Author of *Why Wait? Be Happy Now*

'There is valuable wisdom and authenticity in this empowering book, *Extraordinary You*. This book is an asset to anyone interested in personal growth, self-exploration and/or inspiration. I also find the suggestions at the end of each chapter insightful and useful. You will be giving yourself an amazing gift by reading *Extraordinary You!*'

~ **KATE HEARTSONG**
Speaker and Author of *Deeply We Are One*, Contributing Author to
Speaking Your Truth - Inspiring Stories by Courageous Women

'Every once in a while a book comes your way that wakes your soul with inspiring insights of life, love, and gratitude. *Extraordinary You* is one of those books. A book that makes you believe that anything is possible when we listen to the wisdom of our souls and follow the dreams of our hearts.'

~ **CHRISTIAN MARCHEGIANI**
CEO *THUMP Boxing International*

'What does every human being want from a religion or a spiritual practice? The experience of feeling more alive! *Extraordinary You* delivers just that experience through the vibrant stories of eleven extraordinary people. If you want to feel more alive - read this book!'

~ **JOE ZARANTONELLO**
Director of Looseleaf Hollow Retreat Centre, Author of *Green Bamboo, Mala,* and *Joe's Place*

'A true demonstration of the highest understanding of the Aquarian Age - Together, these women offer us insight, wisdom and compassion for our personal journeys, inspiring us to be our best for the whole of humanity at this pivotal time in history.'

~ **LINDA HOWE**
Spiritual Teacher, Author of *Healing Through the Akashic Records: Using the Power of Your Sacred
Wounds to Discover Your Soul's Perfection* and *How to Read the
Akashic Records: Accessing the Archive of the Soul and its Journey*

'*Extraordinary You* is a sacred account of 11 great souls yearning to live the lives they were meant to live. It is a testament to the resilience and awakening of the human spirit. These stories of transformation offer guidance and inspiration, sure to illuminate the Divine in the life of readers.'

~ **APRIL MARTINO**
Healing Practitioner

Extraordinary You:
The Art of Living a Lusciously Spirited, Vibrant Life
Copyright © Vanessa Talbot-Varian 2011
www.extraordinaryyoubook.com

Vanessa Talbot Photograph: © Lyndal Photography *www.lyndalphotography.com*
Ghania Dib Photograph: © Dayna Patterson, Catchlight Pictures *www.catchlightpictures.com*
Maria Russo Photograph: © Jill Doherty Photography *www.jilldohertyphotography.com*

First published in Australia 2011 by The Publishing Queen
www.thepublishingqueen.com

ISBN 978-1-921673-54-2

Jodie, shine!

I shine light along the path of the unknown for myself and others.

Love + blessings to you!

Asia

Extraordinary YOU

The Art of Living a Lusciously Spirited, Vibrant Life

VANESSA TALBOT

along with ten powerful voices:

Asia Voight • Camile Araujo • Minda Lennon
Leila Khani • Maria Russo • Ghania Dib • Sue Crosbie
Cynthia Zeki • Cath Edwards • Bianca Carroll

DEDICATION

*To all those who dare to dream
that life can be an adventure filled with
magic beyond the wildest of imaginings ...*

And to all those who dare to live it.

CONTENTS

The Keys

Introduction

Why do some people live Extraordinary lives, seemingly illuminated in perpetual happiness and excitement for all that life brings ... while many of us don't? Why do some seem to enjoy such an array of vivid experiences, bathing daily in a shower of love and appreciation from family, friends, partners and strangers alike ... yet the lives of many of us seem dull, colourless in comparison, lacking in brilliance?

'Depression' seems such an accepted and expected word these days. And I couldn't count how many times I've heard the expression 'I'm bored' uttered from young and middle-aged mouths alike. The young express it either with disdain for their surroundings or situations, or with proudness as a badge of honour to differentiate themselves from the rest of us. Meanwhile, the middle-aged will express their dissatisfaction with life by running off with a new obsession that's twenty-five years younger, or by throwing in their job and family to 'go find myself' in a meditation retreat for a year. Though the elderly don't tend to utter the word depression, they too will display it through their daily actions ... or *in-actions* ... that speak so plainly of their lost interest in life.

Expectations are high of what is to be done with the life you are given, with the words 'goals', 'achievements', 'prosperity' and 'success' at the forefront of this modern age all setting benchmarks of attainment. None of these are bad. In fact, I use the word 'success' in my own coaching practice. However, when we do what most of society does and allow these words to become the masters of our focus, they become debilitating, rather than be the helpful, loyal servants they are meant to be as they work silently in the background to improve our lifestyle, not our lives.

Many are living a comfortable, yet tedious existence, tolerating a life devoid of fulfilment. This is especially common in women because of our self-sacrificing nature. It doesn't have to be this way. You have complete control over how you see your Life to be. It's your choice. It's all up to you.

I live an amazingly fulfilling life. But it wasn't always that way, as you will see when you read my chapter. As for every other contributing author, they too are now living extraordinary lives that were once far from it.

So, what's the Big Secret to living a Spirited, Luscious, Vibrant and Extraordinary Life full of excitement and vitality?

I gathered together eleven voices that I felt had something outstanding to say, each voice speaking of a unique key to the Big Secret. The authors in this book share with you their personal stories of discovery toward a more fulfilling life. These Wisdom Guides have all had varying life experiences that led them to see there was more to life than what they were experiencing. They each made a discovery that enabled them to embrace life far greater than they had before.

For many of these Wisdom Guides, they came to a point in their lives where they turned a corner. Whether by force or by constructed choice, they began to live their lives differently to how they had before. Their vision for themselves, and the world around them, was expanded and Life began to magnify to something far more than what it was ever going to be before. For some the turning point was what appeared as tragedy at the time; for others it was a realisation that something had to change. For some it jumped at them ... for others it crept up over time.

What they have learnt, they have each offered in this book as a loving message for you. You can take all these messages on board, or just a few; but what all have in common is that you don't have to jump out of aeroplanes or live in mansions by the sea to live an exhilarating, happy life of magnificence.

This is not a book to race through and then put down, forgotten. It is a book to settle into and reflect upon. You may want to explore a chapter a week, for example, as each chapter contains a unique message – a key toward unlocking an Extraordinary Life. Some messages may seem especially written just for you ... and some may not. With those you feel a connection with, I hope that you will allow yourself special time to reside in and absorb the suggestions and insights that are given for you to explore. Then as you begin to apply the wisdom, rejoice in the difference that is being made to your everyday life – and I assure you there will be a difference.

There is a common trait amongst those who take their lives to outstanding levels of Joy, and that is appreciation. You can live a wonderful life on true, heart-felt appreciation alone. Each contributor in this book, however, has an extra key they have discovered within their own lives to share with you. Before you begin to explore the messages within this book, it is important to note to yourself right now that it is essential to take action on what you are guided to learn. Change doesn't happen by itself. It takes active, willing, eager and patient participation on your behalf to bring down the internal barriers and allow your Real Self to climb through. 'To Be' by actively doing, in the most gentle and loving way, is the most precious gift you can give your Real Self. Take the time to practice this art – the Art of Living a Lusciously Spirited, Vibrant Life as you dwell, explore and discover your way throughout this book.

So, in the spirit of living extraordinarily, I give you eleven keys to creating an exceptional Life.

ENJOY!

Vanessa Talbot

'Every day is a Big opportunity to find
the little things that count ...
it is the little things, when all put
together, that make up a life.'

Vanessa Talbot

Enjoying abundance in all areas of her life – an abundance of Love, Time, Money, Freedom, Fun and Passion – Vanessa is blessed to have as her 'reality' a wonderful life on a country property with the man of her dreams, her beautiful five-year-old daughter, her other 'kids' (four gorgeous ponies), and the wildlife and nature that surrounds them.

A Certified Life and Performance Coach, NLP Practitioner, Matrix Therapist, Author, Presenter, Motivational Speaker AND, to add extra zing to the credentials, an Australian Wildlife Carer, Vanessa has an extraordinary awareness of what it truly means to be alive. The force behind the Living Extraordinarily movement, Vanessa shares through her daily blog, The Year of Living Extraordinarily, the truth about expanding experience and living the life you truly desire by sharing the magic of the everyday.

She believes in success on your own terms ... and knows it is within everyone's essence to achieve it with ease. Vanessa teaches this empowering message via her coaching practice, Extraordinary Beings – Personal Success Creation, an inspirational and transformational coaching service designed to empower people to discover their own unique version of success ... and then create and live it! With her Writers Success Creation, she provides a proactive service for guiding and energising Inspirational, Motivational, Self-help and Spiritual authors to write their book, have it published and build an audience to ensure the book sells.

Vanessa is the author and compiler of *Extraordinary YOU ... The Art of Living a Lusciously Spirited, Vibrant Life* and the forthcoming book, *The Year of Living Extraordinarily,* to be released mid-2012. She successfully coaches and mentors clients across both Australia and the USA in Living Extraordinarily so that their aspirations for Life and Success are no longer dreams but a Reality.

It's the Little Things that Make Life BIG

VANESSA TALBOT

Many live blinded by their To-Do list, erratic schedules and the 'what's coming up next', unable to see the simple beauty of what surrounds them every day. Life is a continuous race of striving but never truly arriving because each attainment is just never enough. We race through our days attempting to get everything done, our tunnel vision locked on the end result, only to fall down at the end of the day exhausted and unsatisfied, even mad at ourselves, because we didn't get all accomplished on the never-ending list. We miss seeing the ordinary moments that we pass through for what they truly are – extraordinary – if we allow them to be so.

Having it All

I was the poster child for having it all. I lived on a country property on the outskirts of town with my husband. Sharing our land were my five beautiful ponies that were also like my children, along with an abundance of wildlife that were accustomed to our presence: kangaroos, possums and a variety of native birdlife.

I had money – more than enough to live an extremely comfortable existence. There was plenty to play with and to spend on clothes and shoes. Ooohhh – especially shoes. I had shoes lining up against the walls in my house as there was no room left in the wardrobes. A lot of them I'd never even worn. I am a country girl after all and the need for sky-high platforms and stilettos and Dolce and Gabbana boots was slim to say the least. Basically, I lived in the same old jeans or tracksuit pants and wellington boots or sandshoes while having a wardrobe of mainly unworn fancy clothes and designer shoes.

Aside from the clothes, there were the expensive beauty products – the Botox to erase frown lines and Juvederm to pump up my lips – all to give me a line-free appearance and boost my confidence by making me look ten years younger. I obsessed over my looks and my weight, both of which were fine, but I was never satisfied or happy with either. Hence, the personal trainer three days a week!

There was no expense spared when it came to the horses and my other pets. The horses got the smartest, classiest horse float, custom-made just for them. I shopped for investment properties as a place to put the excess money. And most of all there were the holidays! I lived to plan my holidays, of which we had three or four a year – trips to far-off places both within Australia and overseas.

I could spend and have what I wanted as price was never an issue. You see, my husband and I had built our business from zero to a multi-million dollar income company within two years – with me working only three afternoons a week and he only one week a month!! On that schedule, I had a lot of time to play.

Which I did.

As I said: holidays, investments, cosmetic procedures, clothes and shoes, and a lot of self-care in diet and exercising to keep my body looking good. And most importantly, because I worked so little and success had come easily, I had lots of quiet time to myself to meditate, to volunteer to nurse back to health sick wildlife and to be with my precious ponies, who above anything else were what made me feel good .

In all, I was living the good life … for a while at least.

What if my Whole Life has Been Wrong?

The truth is, the more the business grew, the more it began to take over our lives. After that initial two years of high-powered growth with little effort, the business began to demand more of our time and take over our easygoing life. Though to outside eyes we had it made, my husband started to become stressed with the more difficult clients as we grew more and more, and I found myself having to spend not just those three afternoons a week in the office but be available at all times. I was doing quotes up at midnight to get through to an overseas client, and my days began to increase in the office, not just on the business but on the management of our personal investments that had started eating into my time. The more money we made, it seemed the more time it took to manage it. I was spending less time playing with my ponies and being outside. Then I had a baby and my life completely changed. The spare moments out of the office were no longer my own.

It looked as if I had it all … the truth was … I was dying inside.

I began to resent the time I had to spend in the office. I questioned what I was doing, cooped up in there all the time when I wanted to be outside with my horses or caring for wildlife. I didn't even like doing all that office administration 'stuff'. Accounts, emails, quotes, payroll, non-stop data entry and managing the cash flow. It was alright in the small amounts when we first started as I still had plenty of time for me. But now it seemed like my life was consumed by it. Even if I wasn't in the office, I was always thinking about what had to be done next! … I was no longer living in the 'now', but in the 'what has to be done next'.

I was no longer living in the 'now', but in the 'what has to be done next'.

At no time did I ever resent my little daughter, but between having a new baby and the office work to do I began to lose sight of me. I thought that as my baby grew I would get my time back, but it never happened. There just seemed to be more to do every step of the way. And I never lost the baby weight because I had stopped exercising, finding I didn't have the time. I had to stop taking in the orphaned and injured wildlife as I just couldn't care for them and my daughter and do all the business work at the same time.

As I began to get more and more frustrated with the loss of my easygoing, relaxed life, to attempt to ease this frustration I spent. More shoes, more Botox, more houses. It took a toll on my husband as well. He too was suffering with the load of dealing with big-name clients that we couldn't really afford to lose, even though he would have liked to erase his stress by telling them where to go. But we couldn't get rid of the troublesome contracts because our big financial situation demanded that we continue to make and bring in big money. It's a never-ending circle. The more you earn, the more you need to continue to earn. He could see that I was losing myself as well. He tried to talk me into getting an office assistant to take off the load. I'd tried a couple in the earlier days and had found the process a dismal failure, so I wouldn't have any of it. I couldn't let that control go and put the business admin in the hands of someone else. So, I chose instead to die inside, just to retain the sense of control I had over the finances and the way things were run and done.

I'm going to take you back a little here, to before I made lots of money and before I had every moment of the day allotted and accounted for. Back to when I was younger. To when I had dreams.

I wanted to write. Movies. I wanted to be a scriptwriter and win an Academy Award for best original screenplay. I wanted to see my story up on the big screen with famous actors playing the parts. I did a scriptwriting course to learn the craft. I was good, apparently. According to my tutor and mentor that had worked in the industry for years, I was damn good. So much so that he hired me to work on his own show. I wrote two screenplays of my own, and in a month-long flurry of creativity that just came to me I wrote a novel as well. The novel came to be short-listed for a prestigious award that year, and because of that status I had contacts from literary luminaries offering to work with me. I was runner-up in the romantic fiction story of the year award at the time. My family would tell me that writing must be in my blood; that I take after another family member, British playwright Noel Coward. (My grandfather's cousin and my great-grandmother's nephew) I did a stint writing articles for a youth publication, though that wasn't my passion. I wanted to be a screenplay luminary and novelist.

That novel and the screenplays are still sitting in my office drawer. Never published. Somewhere along the way, as I embarked on the new business venture with my husband, I lost my dream and I didn't think I wanted to write anymore. In the early stages of the business, the first two years when time was still mine, I instinctively knew I wanted more out of life.

That's when I joined a wildlife group and began caring for sick, injured or orphaned wildlife. It made me feel whole, that I was giving and helping something else in this world. I also knew I didn't want to be doing the boring office admin and running the business my entire time. I wanted to be doing something of greater interest for me. Maybe work with animals, or perhaps even something inspirational like helping people discover how to get the most from their lives. But as the business grew and more money came in, those ideas flew out of my mind, being suffocated by the continuing profit that I became obsessed with growing and growing year after year.

My life became a never-ending life of being in the office. To give myself any sign of relief from that tedium, I would plan big, elaborate holidays. That's where my excitement came from. If I didn't have the holidays to plan and look forward to, and the thrill of going out and buying stuff, I would've been lost in the mundane.

I was so busy being a Wife, a Mother and a Successful Business Owner that I forgot about Me. I was existing. Oh yes, I was existing very well all right. But I wasn't truly living – living for me.

I was so busy being a Wife, a Mother and a Successful Business Owner that I forgot about Me.

My frustration became so strong that I could no longer sleep at night. I began to realise that no matter how much I had it 'good', there were parts of my life that were not right. Life had taken a completely different direction to what I had once imagined. I had imagined I would shine as an author or Academy Award winner, having a bountiful amount of spare time to spend with animals. Instead, I had a successful business, but no matter how successful it was, the fact was I was seen as just an appendage to my husband's brilliance; I was just the office girl. Of course, I knew that not to be true. I was as much a driving force behind the success of the business with my money management skills, but I had received opposition to my vision for the business from my husband. And, the fact is, it ended up being run on his vision not mine. Hence, I was running someone else's vision, living someone else's dream, even though the pay-off for me was spectacularly good in financial terms. I eventually began to feel I was not being heard by my husband, and the relationship for this reason began to suffer.

My baby daughter, who grew to a toddler and then a pre-schooler in this time, was missing out on serious mummy playtime as I kept telling her, 'Not now, I'm working', every time she came in to ask me to play. My horses were missing out on their time, as well, as I was racing out each evening for only half an hour to pick up the manure rather than spending time actually bonding with them. I even gave up the wildlife caring as I told myself I didn't have time anymore.

I was so driven by my financial life that I wasn't coming up for air. I spent one entire winter unwell, yet still pushed on, unwilling to rest from all the work I had to do. 'It's just the cold winter making me feel so down and blue', I would tell myself. 'In springtime I will feel better'. And springtime came ... and nothing! I was still feeling constantly run down and yet never stopping to take rest. During that Spring November, while in Melbourne on business for a week, I was surprised on the first day to hear so many people tell me that I looked unwell. I felt fine. I couldn't really see it, though my body did feel a little lethargic. In my mind, I was raring to go. By day two, I couldn't drag myself out of bed. I was determined to make the training that I had flown down to Melbourne for, so I found a doctor that morning in the apartment building I was staying at, hoping he'd give me something to pick me up enough to head right back to my seminar.

'You're not going anywhere for at least a week,' was the news. 'You have pneumonia and it looks like you've been battling it for a long time.'

Pneumonia! I couldn't believe it!

'No,' I demanded. 'I need to get back to my training – now.'

'The only way you'll get back to it this week is if I pump you up with a massive dose of steroids, and even then you still have to rest for the next two days.' I settled for that option because even though I liked the feel of constantly pushing myself, I knew inside that I really needed to rest, and I could allow myself at least two days (but not a week!).

Two days alone in a hotel room in a strange city, sick and unwell, gives you a lot of time to think. What I thought about was the track I was heading down. While I was focusing on the future, and all the extravagances that even more money would be buying me, I wasn't enjoying my days.

I was living for the future.

I wasn't living for now.

I looked back down that track I'd already trudged and recognised that I hadn't been spending the quality time with my daughter that I should have, or out there enjoying my quiet meditative moments with my ponies like I used to, or volunteering as a wildlife carer as I had planned. Instead, I had been telling myself, 'If I can just get the business to where I want it to be then I can rest and settle back into the peaceful, serene life I truly love.' I was waiting to get to a point in the business where I could be free to concentrate on what I loved doing. But the fact of the matter was I'd been saying this for years, and every year the business made more, and yet it still wasn't, in my eyes, at the place where I could say, 'That's enough!' What I realised then was that it never would be …

While I was focusing on the future, and all the extravagances that even more money would be buying me, I wasn't enjoying my days.

Day after day I had been sitting in that office doing work I disliked, and when I was finally free, my beautiful daughter occupied the rest of my time, the little of it there was. And to top it all off, because of my own inner turmoil, I had lost my connection with my husband due to my loss of connection with myself.

I had lost me.

In that hotel room I truly didn't know if when I got to the end of my life and had to face the question 'What if my whole life has been wrong?' I would be able to say with assuredness that it hadn't been. In fact, I knew the answer would have been that had been.

Something had to change.

Reclaiming Me

That day in the hotel room was the day I decided to reclaim me. On my return home a few days later, I gave up my directorship and ownership and walked away from the business. A woman was hired to take my place running the business and administration side of things. It was really, REALLY hard to let go of something I had controlled for so long, even though inside I was burning to. And so, when reality came and I walked away from that office, slipping it all into her hands, I felt an immense sense of loss. Something that I had built from nothing and watched grow, like a child, I was to have nothing more to do with. It also meant I had nothing to hide behind anymore and the rest of my life was clear to see – dismal.

So there I was. No longer a big business owner. No longer with any income. Or with a husband to support me – for when I gave up the business, the husband went too. All of a sudden I was faced with the fact that I basically had my life to start over again.

A fresh new start.

The thing about fresh new starts is that they can be very scary to begin with. What if my fresh new start and any fresh new ideas were to fail? I felt I was leaping off a cliff with absolutely no clue where I was going to land.

It would have been easy to dismiss it all as unobtainable and just a silly dream.

What I did know, though, was that the earlier dream I had squashed of having a book out there had quickly reappeared after being pushed away for so long. But this time it was in a slightly different way. It was no longer about novels and movie writing; I felt more inclined toward being a wisdom guide. After years and years of having an interest in personal development and the inspirational field, of learning the lessons, accessing my intuition and getting in touch with my inner me – then abandoning it all to the lure of financial reward – I felt I had something to teach. It came to me that I wanted to write transformational books, to guide and help others to find their own true place in life. And I wanted to keep on making lots of money as well. A Hay House author speaking at the Hay House 'I can do it' event was sounding good to me! Lofty ideas for a country girl in regional Australia. It would have been easy to dismiss it all as unobtainable and just a silly dream. But I had spent the last fifteen years abandoning my dreams. This time, even though they differed slightly now, I had a reason to shoot for the stars.

The reason was ... this time I was bare.

No business to build. No glittering distractions to keep me from being authentically me.

With my first foray into the writing business all those years ago, I knew enough to be aware that I wasn't going to get Hay House (or anyone else for that matter) to publish my book without having some credibility behind me. Apart from a lifelong interest, I had no active experience in the motivational field. Yet I knew I was passionate about it and had been so for a long time. So, what could I do about it? I remembered back to eight years earlier, when life had been slower and easier and I would take lunch outside to my front verandah every day. Leisurely hour-long lunches where I would read a self-help magazine as I ate. On one such day, I flicked through a spiritual newspaper and an advertisement for training to be a life coach caught my eye. The idea had immediately interested me at the time.

Even though by that stage I hadn't heard of a life coach before, 'inspiring others to success, to reaching their full potential and living out their personal dreams' sounded good to me. I'd be good at that; I just knew. BUT, then the BUTs came in. *You've got this business to build. You should be concentrating on that, not scattering your energy elsewhere.* That did make sense. Okay. I would build the business and then, when I had it where I wanted it to be, I would be free to go off and do this life coaching stuff.

Of course, I never became free to go off and do this coaching 'stuff'. In fact, I even stopped being able to take long lunches on my front verandah. I stopped doing a lot of the things I used to enjoy.

So, here I was, eight years later. And after having thrown it all in – the marriage, the business – following my return from that two day soul searching session in that lonely hotel room in a strange city ... I had no income. None at all ... and wondering how I was going to make this 'follow your dreams' thing work. Contemplating how to get my name out there as a personal development expert, I recalled that life coaching advertisement from those leisurely lunch days so long ago. Strangely enough, I even remembered who the coaching school was that had placed the ad. I could do that. I could coach. I could guide others toward the financial success I had achieved. That way I would have income doing something I enjoyed, while working on this motivational author 'thing'.

Right then and there I rang the school and pretty much signed up immediately. This was the beginning of making my life resemble what I had once intended it to be.

What I discovered when embarking on my new path towards my dream was that there was also to be a new 'me'. I'd always been very shy from childhood, right through to my adult life. My shyness came off not as a quaint character trait of endearment, but rather as aloofness, even snobbiness. Certainly unsociable. But I know I was neither aloof nor a snob. In fact, I think I was also seen as being a little sour by some because they thought I never smiled. Well, I did smile ... when I would feel the loving nudge of my pony's muzzle in my ear, or held a baby bird in my hands and felt the gratification and relief of finally getting it to eat, for then I knew it would thrive. Around nature and the simple pleasures of life, I smiled a lot.

My shyness came off not as a quaint character trait of endearment, but rather as aloofness, even snobbiness.

To be a life coach, first I had to learn how to coach. At my first three-day intake classes for my training in life coaching I was terrified to be surrounded by all these new faces. It frightened me to walk into the room every morning for the class. It was all so unfamiliar to me, having to be with all these new people that, maybe, would all be so much better than me.

But a funny thing happened. As I continued my coaching journey, attended more training, met more and more people, secured clients and then became well known for my success coaching, I found myself being seen in a way that I had never seen myself before – as the one who is always optimistic and vivacious, with high energy levels that fly through the roof! I heard the comments on many occasions after leaving a meeting that my energy was so highly refreshing and uplifting. Not only was I adding some spark to myself, I was beginning to add spark elsewhere. As I allowed my own self to take flight, I would see others' eyes change before my very own as they too were filled with the magic of possibilities. It seemed so sudden to now become to all these new eyes the natural, high energy, transformational girl that had eternal optimism to boot.

So, how does a woman who was seen as snobby, unsociable and aloof to all eyes, seemingly overnight become a vehicle of all-natural optimism and uplifting energy, drawing people with her (quote) 'beautiful smile'? Never in a million years would I think that person would be me. But it was. It is. I can only respond that the answer must be because she is living with passion for her dreams.

Even though I still have quite a way to go to reaching the best-selling inspirational author status I aspire to, I am actively living the journey toward my dream – to all of my dreams – because that is only one of them. The passion now boils inside me, bursting at the seams, whereas before, when I was toiling away at the administrative work I really didn't like, passion didn't even come close to a simmer.

The difference between the flying and the just living is only one thing: Living with the passion of actively creating my dreams.

I have not yet obtained all I wish to, but I am living proof that even in the act of moving toward what you truly want for your life, knowing that each day is a step closer (even if at times you feel it's not), an essence of joyful expectation will radiate from you and draw others, along with opportunities, toward you in a synergistic way that brings more and more vibrancy to you every day. The difference I have experienced between flying on even just a prayer and hope and just living day after day with no hope is immense. I have made connections, had new opportunities and taken risks that I would never have dreamed of before, even with all the previous money I made. And the difference between now and then – the difference between the flying and the just living – is only one thing:

Living with the passion of actively creating my dreams and carving my future every day.

It doesn't even matter if I never get to be the next Wayne Dyer or Louise Hay. Because by God I'm having fun along the way.

Though now I have far more creative exploits to develop and explore, it doesn't mean that my time is now completely free. On my new adventure,

I work just as hard as I had previously in the office for my successful mine contracting business. But the difference is it doesn't feel like such a self-sacrificing slog. Now, the vision is mine. And the work is towards my big vision. **I am living on purpose ... not just existing without one.**

For this time, I'm not letting my dreams slip away from me again. But in saying that, I'm also not going to make the same mistake. That hell-bent-driven-for-success-at-whatever-cost life without passion had been the mistake. This time, along my pathway to success I'm going to do it differently. And this is how.

Every day is a BIG Opportunity to Find the Little Things that Count!

What I have to tell you next was the most important step of all to my now living a lusciously spirited, vibrant life. On my immediate return home from those dark days of soul searching in a hotel room, it wasn't throwing in the work and business I was unhappy doing, or ending a marriage I felt emotionally stilted in, that I did first. Nor were they the moves that were to have the biggest impact for bringing joy back into my life. It was far simpler.

It was this: The moment I stepped back into my house on my return from the Melbourne business seminar, I took my little daughter in my arms and told her about 'Lucia Time'. You see, Lucia is her name. Lucia Time was to be an hour every evening, just for her. Doing anything she wanted to with Mummy. It was her choice as to what we would do and I, Mummy, was not allowed to say no. One special hour together every late afternoon, just for me and her.

What I have to tell you next was the most important step of all to my now living a lusciously spirited, vibrant life.

I walked outside and made the promise to my horses to spend far more time with them again; to let them out of their paddocks and onto the house lawn as we used to years before so that they could rest at the back door, peak through the kitchen windows, eat the rose bushes, and gallop to the front gate and back while kicking up their hooves. And I would brush them. Oh yes, I'd brush them again and feel their soft fur under my hand,

and be with them outside on a beautiful day as they graze while I read.

I made the promise to myself to stop limiting my food to diet food in an effort to lose weight. All the diet food over the last five years wasn't making any difference at all, and if I got back to exercising again like I once did, I could go back to eating glorious food. I would cook something gooey and calorie-laden every weekend for us to enjoy a sumptuous feast. Without guilt. No remorse. I would go out to dinner whenever anyone asked me to, instead of saying 'no' for fear of pigging out on solid food that was more than lean protein and lettuce leaves.

I would run again like I used to. Run and feel my feet spring on the bitumen road beneath. Run as I cleared my head and allowed all the muck to drain out, returning with nothing but brilliant ideas no longer smudged in cloud. And if I didn't run, I would at least walk for an hour every day. Walk and listen and watch all the birds that line my road. Make friends with them once again, with every one of them like I used to. I would rejoice when they had their newborn chicks each spring and weep when I would find the occasional one squashed by a motorist on the road.

I would take on a wild creature to nurture and care for. Just one, or maybe two, so that I could give and contribute to the care of our world. After that particular decision, only two days later a young female hawk, a little Nankeen Kestrel, appeared on my back lawn, battered and wounded after a hail storm. I swooped her up into my arms, and once again I immediately felt the sheer joy of nursing one of our precious wild creatures back to health in the hope of returning her back to nature where she belongs. I was needed. I was doing one of the things I was meant to be doing. Back to caring for nature, even if only in a small way.

I also bought a beautiful journal, and each evening in it I would write one thing, just one little thing, that had brought me joy that day. These are some of my entries:

> 'Jasmine my pony's birthday today. She turns six. Gave a little birthday lunch for us all and the ponies had cake and homemade bread. My gorgeous kids. And Lucia sang them Happy Birthday. So cute.'

> 'Watched the movie 'Seven Pounds' tonight. So beautiful.

Made me go outside and think of life. And that was beautiful sitting outside in the dark quiet night.'

'I love the way my Lucia kisses me of her own accord, or wraps herself around my leg and kisses it.'

'Sat out in the barn and read a little this afternoon, just me and my ponies. Beauty snoring behind me, Jasmine's head on my shoulder. Bliss!'

'Lovely little bat in my house tonight. How and when he got inside I don't know. Put him outside and had a little pat.'

'Playing in the park on this icy cold day with Lucia. No work done, but she is happy, excited and full of love.'

'Good to see Squiddly duck and her seven babies down the dam. She takes them from one dam to the other around here. Poor little buggers must get sore legs on the long walks. They are so cute, especially when they are peeping out of their hidey place in the log at me.'

'Snow is falling. I watch from my office window as it floats on by and carpets the land white. Magical.'

Out of all the changes I made, this one – writing one simple moment that stood out each day – was to have the most effect. It taught me, even on the really bad days when nothing seemed to go right, to look for the something that was. It taught me to find peace and joy and wisdom and gratitude for every day. Most of all, it taught me to look beyond the future and back to the 'now'.

To find the joy in the everyday.

In the little things.

I learnt that every day is a BIG opportunity to find the little things that count. I learnt that it is the little things, when all put together, that make up a life. Not the big mountainous goals that we struggle and strive to meet, and when we get there, yes, it's exhilarating. Yet it is not the few moments of achievements that we should be celebrating, rather all the small moments that make for a BIG life.

Now, every day is my passion. My coaching business built steadily. You are reading the first of my books right now. I stay at home in my own little private paradise and work the hours of my choosing doing something I enjoy. If my daughter wants to play down at the local playground, and it's a beautiful day outside, I am able to grab her by the hand and say, 'YES!' instead of all the 'NOs' she would hear before.

Vanessa's BIG life with one of the little things that count: Taffy, one of her horses.

I feel as I have made no sacrifices in daring to walk my own path of joy. The loss I felt a year ago from giving up my previous company has now long faded and gone, replaced with a sense of gratitude that I was able to learn over ten years such amazing business skills – a sense of pride that I took the plunge. And time quickly proved it to be the right choice.

I don't need holidays to add excitement and adventure to my life anymore, for every day, with all the little joys, is something to look forward to. Don't get me wrong, though. I still love the adventure of travelling and my curiosity and fascination for all things new will still take me to far flung shores. But now I no longer see holidays as the only excitement I have to look forward to.

I sleep like a nineteen-year-old cat. I rise each morning, eager for the day. And though every day is similar – I rise anytime between 7 am and 9 am. I go out to yell across the lawn 'Good morning!' to my ponies. I make myself a slow, relaxing breakfast, and I enjoy it in a slow, relaxing mode. No rush. I meditate for half an hour. Then I put on my running shoes and I pound, or walk, the track I live on and feel the fresh air stimulate my senses. I am back on name basis with the birds that I pass by every day. The magpies across the road have had a new baby. This morning, I picked him off the road and put him back high in a tree. My afternoons are as serene as I want them to be, or as flurried as I care to let them be. I write, I market, I create. I meet with clients and help them surrender to their own dreams and ambitions without ever having to leave my front door, for Skype is a wonderful thing. Or else I lay back with a magazine and do little else – every day delivers joy.

As I write this, a young female kangaroo, who I raised from a baby, lies on my front lawn with her own baby in pouch now. Lying next to her, totally relaxed in this environment of peace, is her 'boyfriend', a young male that has taken to calling her his own. She is happy to have kangaroo company without having to leave home.

I have settled into an easier way of being. I am no longer just existing, but truly living the success that is unique to me ... just me.

At this moment, my ponies graze also on my front lawn. They are happy to once again be able to wreak havoc on the rose garden, race up and down the driveway and come when I call their names.

I live in abundance: an abundance of time, love, passion. And I still like shoes! I just don't buy so many now.

I have settled into an easier way of being. I am no longer just existing, but truly living the success that is unique to me ... just me. My exuberance for life now radiates for all to see.

I'm not waiting to be a well-known, successful inspirational author before I am living the life of my dreams. I now find every ordinary day rich and tantalising. I do not know the meaning of the word 'bored'. I have an ordinary, quiet life ... yet it feels so much more.

It feels extraordinary.

To me.

Finding the Extraordinary in You

I took the long road to discovering that the little daily joys are what feed an extraordinary life. You don't have to. If your life is feeling routine, stale, you don't have to take massive jumps out of your comfort zone to jazz it up. It truly is so often as simple as looking for the magic in your every day. And the world has a way of rewarding us when we begin to open our eyes and look. It rewards us with more and more, and even more, of all the good stuff that we have suddenly opened our awareness to. All those 'New Agers' don't go on about the sheer transformational delight and magic of a sunset, or a twilight walk on the beach, without it being true. It's all about the simple things, such as picking fresh fruit and then making it into something divine to eat, walking a spring day path while feeling the new warm sun on your shoulders, seeing the first season baby ducklings daring to swim, watching the dandelion seeds float by on the breeze. And reading your child a bedtime story every night.

> *The moment that matters most is the moment you are in now – for every moment is what makes up a life.*

So many people spend years of anxiety about finding their purpose in life. As they ache and stress that life is passing them by and focus on a future that is yet to exist, they forget about finding their happiness in the present. They think they cannot be happy, for their purposeful future is not yet here.

But they can be happy. YOU can choose to be happy.

Life is a journey that's not about the destination. The moment that matters most is the moment you are in now – for every moment is what makes up a life.

Not the future or the past.

It is every little moment.

So, it is in those everyday moments that you will find your joy. You will find your extraordinary life, quite unlike anyone else's. It's when you truly make the decision to live these moments with mindfulness and joy that you will discover You.

And by discovering You, your purpose and passions will find you. And you can live them all, just as I do.

When a person is near the end of his life, any regrets he may have are never about how he didn't spend enough time at work, or earn enough money, or drive a Lamborghini. They are that he never spent enough time with his loved ones, or enjoyed his children before they grew up, or took the time to do the things he really longed to do. He never spent enough time to just BE.

I made the decision to live an ordinary life in an extraordinary way by bringing back the simple joys into my life, the little passions that I enjoy.

I now follow my inner self, allowing my spirit to rejoice at each day of experiencing my aspirations coming true, trusting all will be in the right timing for me, instead of putting my life on hold as I frantically chase the dream down and force it to come true. I have opened my eyes to the world I already have and stopped chasing blindly the world I am yet to obtain.

By living immersed in the magic of the every day, and by finally allowing my inner self to do what it knew it was always meant to do, I feel more successful now than ever before, enjoying every moment, every step in the dance that is Life.

At the very beginning of my journey to this sparkling life of fun and adventure and passion that I enjoy at my own back door, I came across this passage by an eighty-five year old lady named Nadine Stair on looking back over her life. It is from the book *Condensed Chicken Soup for the Soul* by Jack Canfield, Mark Victor Hansen and Patty Hansen, and it put everything into perspective for me. This was a pivotal point in my opening up to living a Lusciously Spirited, Vibrant and Extraordinary Life and to explore and dwell in the magic of everyday.

I would like to share it with you here.

If I Had My Life to Live Over [1]

I'd dare to make more mistakes next time.
I'd relax. I would limber up.
I would be sillier than I have been this trip.
I would take fewer things seriously.
I would take more chances.
I would take more trips.
I would climb more mountains and swim more rivers.
I would eat more ice cream and less beans.

I would perhaps have more actual troubles but
I'd have fewer imaginary ones.

You see, I'm one of those people who live sensibly
and sanely hour after hour, day after day.

Oh, I've had my moments and if I had it to do over
again, I'd have more of them. In fact,
I'd try to have nothing else. Just moments.

One after another, instead of living so many
years ahead of each day.

I've been one of those people who never go anywhere
without a thermometer, a hot water bottle, a raincoat
and a parachute.

If I had my life to live over, I would start barefoot
earlier in the spring and stay that way later in the fall.

If I had it to do again, I would travel lighter next time.
I would go to more dances.
I would ride more merry-go-rounds.
I would pick more daisies.

---

[1] Nadine Stair (age 85); *Condensed Chicken Soup for the Soul*; Copyright 1996; Jack Canfield, Mark Victor Hansen & Patty Hansen

Suggestions to Help You Live Extraordinarily by Appreciating the Everyday Moments that Make a Life

❀ *Define your existence*

Are you a human do-ing or a human be-ing? Stop filling your day with things to do and busyness. Make sure you have a balance between your To-Do list and time for your own passions and interests; just feel good to Be You. As you read this, make the decision to allow your be-ing to shine through today.

❀ *Create a Joy List*

Wander through a stationery store and immerse yourself in all the beautiful journals. Buy the one that speaks to you. This is to be your **Joy List.** At the end of each day, write down one – it only has to be ONE – aspect of your day that brought you happiness, or made you feel good, or turned your lips into a smile, or gave you immense pleasure or gratification. Your Joy for the Day. Even on the bad days, find that one thing that caused that flutter of joy for you. Maybe a bright orange butterfly fluttered past your nose and rested in the flowers outside. Perhaps your child told you 'I love you', or for just a few seconds, while you watched the sky as it turned purple and pink in a mid-winter sunset, all your cares and worries disappeared.

Just one simple act like these will awaken you to the appreciation of your everyday 'now'. As you get into the habit, you will begin to unconsciously look for the good things that surround you and that happen to you. And over time you will always be in a state of expectation that every day will provide you with wonderful experiences to look forward to. And as the Law of Attraction states, when you focus on something, it comes. This one simple act will change the way you see your life. And as you move into the expectations of your life being a wonderful, spirited, vibrant existence, your life will become just that.

Get back to basics

We live in a modern world but too often we pay the price for our success and technology by living a burned-out, stressful life. Bring some romance and nostalgia into your life by welcoming some simple but immensely soul satisfying basics back into your life. Pick blackberries from a wild bush and bake them into a pie – one you've made from scratch all by yourself. Feel the satisfaction of those dark, little ripe fruits stain your tongue black. Poke out your tongue for all to see. Packeted food from the supermarket or take-away is quick and convenient, but what is this quick convenience doing?

Begin with just one or two nights a week, and take the time to linger over your food. Cook from scratch; maybe make up a simple, slow-cooking beef stew. Smell the aroma wafting for hours through your home. Eat it slow, savouring every morsel, while having good conversation with friends and family because you've turned off the TV.

And here's another back to basics tip! **Try one night a week without TV.** On TV-free night plan something else that interests you: a book you've long meant to read; playing old-fashioned board games with your kids; maybe learning that craft; or finally doing that course you've always wanted to do. Living extraordinarily is in the simple things of the everyday.

GET YOUR EXTRAORDINARY
FREE GIFT BONUS

Vanessa Talbot is kindly offering a **FREE BONUS GIFT**
to all readers of this book.

101 WAYS TO LIVE EXTRAORDINARILY

A delightful eBook of 101 ways to brighten and lift
your everyday, with tips, suggestions and creative ideas
to add spark to the ordinary ... so you can begin to
live extraordinarily!

Simply visit the web page below and follow the directions
to directly download *101 Ways to Live Extraordinarily.*

www.theyearoflivingextraordinarily.com

'Every time we stop listening to our gut feeling,
we become strangers to ourselves ...
The Voice exists. It is here to guide you.'

Camile F. Araujo

Camile F. Araujo is a retired police officer from the Miami Dade Police Department, USA. She empowers people to live extraordinary lives by teaching them to be grateful for everything they go through – because nothing is wasted in the Universe. Camile has a unique outlook on life as she almost lost her own over five years ago to an automobile accident that left her paralysed from the chest down. After waking up from her six-week induced coma, the first thing she heard was her own inner voice, which guided her to where she is today. Camile's extraordinary outlook has led to her being booked for numerous public speaking engagements where she continues to inspire many people to live grateful and magnificent lives.

Camile's writings have been published in the Australian women's magazine, *Footprints,* and on the website of *www.thisibelieve.org.* She is also a contributor for an online magazine for women in wheelchairs *www.mobileWOMEN.org.* Camile is presently writing her first book – *Journey Beyond Happyville* – due out mid-2012.

As a perpetual student of life, Camile has been searching to understand the meaning of life and Universal Laws, even from the tender, young age of seven. It was not by chance that after having gone through some preparation and understanding in her own life, she met Dr. John F. Demartini, a human behavioural specialist and educator, also founder of The Demartini Institute. Dr. Demartini's philosophy resonated deeply with Camile and she found herself 'at home' for the first time while attending his signature seminar The Breakthrough Experience®. Camile is now a trained Demartini Method® Facilitator. When she is not working with clients, writing, researching or speaking, she is a full time mother to her one-year-old daughter, Anastasia.

The Voice Within

Listen to Your Inner Voice and Discover Your Authentic Self

CAMILE F. ARAUJO

As I sit at my writing desk reflecting over the past five years, I think about the ways my life has dramatically changed. Intervening events or signs have been constants in my life, although I often ignored them along my journey. I recall one of these significant events as if it were yesterday. My cousin and I had had an argument. We were sitting in my living room, she on my army green sofa and me on the matching love seat adjacent to her. The tension between us was thick.

'You are not living your life!' she told me in a quiet yet assertive voice, which I heard instead as a scream.

My response to her was my same response to everything at that time – defensive and stubborn. 'How dare you tell me whether or not I'm living my life!'

She patiently looked at me and replied, 'You are destined for so much more than what you're settling for.' Even though the voice within me echoed her words, I ignored it. My cousin saw through all the facades and tried to reach through to the real me. It was the first time someone called me out on this sensitive subject. I wouldn't have any of it.

From the outside, an onlooker would never have guessed that I had anything wrong with my life. I was a very promising twenty-nine-year-old police officer with the Miami Dade Police Department. I was single, beautiful and independent, and yet I felt guilty for feeling what I was feeling. Even though I fitted the profile that I thought society expected of me, nothing I did filled the void I felt inside. No matter how many miles I ran on the beach, how many arrests I made at work, how much money I spent at the hair salon or shopping mall, or how many self-help books I read, I felt hollow. Everything had become too easy.

I tried to numb the pain that accompanied the feeling of emptiness. I would find temporary relief, but nothing fixed me permanently. I sought instant gratification, and when the gratifying part would end, taking me back to square one, I concealed my inner struggle by repeating the same patterns.

It wasn't the first time life had spoken to me. This was my third sign in a period of three years. I had heard life's whispers before. This time, though, it no longer sounded like a whisper. It was as if someone was shouting directly into my ears. I just chose to put up the volume of my brain and ignore what was being said. The Universe had even petitioned my cousin to speak on its behalf. It didn't work.

The First Time Life Spoke

While I was separating from my husband in 2002, a soft, loving, familiar voice emanating from deep within my heart whispered, 'Pack the essentials and go travel. Quit your job. Trust life. You will be provided for. Go discover new horizons, meet new people and learn new cultures. Time is running out.' Again, I ignored it. Instead, when I got divorced, I didn't quit my police dispatcher job. I stayed put in my city, attached myself to what I already knew and ignored my heart's plea. I applied to become a police officer.

I had met my husband two years after graduating high school. It was at my twentieth birthday party that a childhood friend planned for me. I instantly knew that he and I had connected. I'd been single for a while and was working full time as a receptionist for a multinational corporation, living pay cheque to pay cheque, longing to finish college but lacking the funds to do so. I was living a very stagnant life. Previously an over-achiever, I felt dormant, as if the best of me had been left behind in my high school halls.

My husband-to-be appeared in my life at a time when I didn't know who I truly was. At twenty years old, the only thing I knew for sure was that I wanted my life to flourish into something meaningful. I wanted to travel, meet different people, have life altering experiences and become a perpetual student of life. Most of all, I wanted to be an inspirer. However, I feared pursuing those dreams; I was immobilised by my fear. Shortly after we met, my husband and I began to date and eventually moved in together. I was married at twenty-three.

During my relationship, I buried my innermost dreams inside myself, pretending they didn't exist. That way, I could survive living every day without feeling any regret or resentment. Unfortunately, whatever we suppress in life springs up in a different form somewhere else. I had quit my receptionist job and started working as a police dispatcher. I despised it. I soon blamed my unhappiness on my job. I also withdrew from my childhood friends. At such a young age, I felt decades older.

My husband and I were over-spenders. We lived above our means, and as the main breadwinner I began to resent the overspending. After three years of being married and six and a half years of being with him, I

I buried my innermost dreams inside myself, pretending they didn't exist. That way, I could survive living every day without feeling any regret or resentment.

began to grow tired of living a life fulfilling someone else's dream and not my own. I constantly had the nagging feeling I was in the wrong place, living the wrong life. I never acted upon it, however. I was scared. I often dreamt of the day when I wouldn't have to report my whereabouts to anyone or share what I had worked so hard for; I dreamt of being free. But I was scared of the pain. I didn't want to discover that maybe I was a failure without him, too. Even worse, I feared I wouldn't know how to be 'Camile' without him by my side.

'Be brave. Leave. Trust.'

Those words bombarded my head incessantly, but I froze each time and ignored them. One Saturday, during the summer of 2002, I came back home from work and did not find my husband home as I had expected. It had been months since he and I had spent any quality time together. I only saw him in the mornings as I left for work and sometimes during the weekends. He would arrive late at night from work, hours after I had already gone to sleep, and tried not to be home during the weekend so as not to spend much time with me. It had become a draining cycle. The Friday night before, I fell asleep crying, feeling sorry for myself. I had written in my journal a Dear John letter, which I never intended to give him.

Shortly after I arrived home, he also arrived. 'We need to talk,' he said to me as he walked into our bedroom. I sat on the bed, feeling the weight of discomfort between the two of us. We were two strangers living in the same house. He could hardly look me in the eye as he continued. 'I found this in the garbage this morning. When were you planning on giving it to me?' He handed me a rough draft of the Dear John letter I had written.

'I wasn't planning on giving it to you. It was just something I wrote to relieve the pain I have been feeling inside for the last couple of months,' I replied. He started to cry.

'I love you,' he said, 'but I'm not in love with you anymore. I don't even want to come home at night from work anymore.' He continued to cry.

I looked him in the eye and asked, 'Have you met someone else?'

He said no. 'I want a divorce,' were his final words in that conversation. We divorced three months later. I had accidentally set myself free, but there was still a long way to go.

The Second Warning

When my grandmother passed away from diabetic complications, two and a half years after my divorce, I'd been a probationary police officer for seven months. I missed seeing her alive for the last time by just one week. As I tried to comprehend that she was gone, the same familiar voice arose for the second time and it nagged me for a whole week.

'Quit. Now. It's time to do what you haven't done yet.'

The whirlwind of emotions inside of me were unbearable. I felt as if I was on the verge of a nervous breakdown.

My grandparents were prominent figures in both my brother's life and mine. After losing our father when we were very young, my brother and I were showered by abundant love from our grandparents. It was understood that every Friday afternoon the school bus driver would drop us off at our grandparents' house. Their home provided us with security and love, to say nothing of the many interesting hobbies that occupied my grandfather's time after he retired. He was an amateur filmmaker and photographer, and he had his own darkroom to develop his pictures.

As children we are mostly connected to our inner wisdom.

I have learned over the years that as children we are mostly connected to our inner wisdom. It speaks to us constantly. A child's intuition is a very valuable trait. Children do not judge or second-guess the voice that speaks to them. It was during those days, while in my grandparents' movie room, watching The Sound of Music, The Wizard of Oz or Singing in the Rain, or posing for him in different venues as he tried out his newest cameras, that I heard the Voice for the first time in my life.

'Be a storyteller.'

I knew then that I wanted to write and make movies – quite far-fetched dreams for a little girl from Sao Paulo, Brazil, with no plans to ever go to Hollywood.

Losing my grandmother was like losing part of my history. I felt my dream slip away once more. Again, instead of quitting my job and backpacking all over the world to discover myself, I went on a three-week planned vacation. I travelled to Brazil and spent some much needed time with my family in my grandmother's old house. Those three weeks helped put my 'whispering ghosts' to rest, but seven months later, that dreadful feeling in the pit of my stomach returned.

The words 'What else is there for me to do in life?' started to resound inside my head. Once again, I ignored the Voice to avoid having to act upon my feelings. Life went on as usual – but not for long.

As I tried to ignore the messages from the Voice, I also became aware that something inside me was struggling to wake up. Memories began to come back to me. I remembered my first summer in college at Florida

International University and how much I had surprised myself by loving my English classes. I had always considered myself a left-brained, analytical, mathematically-inclined person. I thought I would end up with a degree in Business or Accounting due to my ease and deep understanding of numbers. But, that summer of 1994, in the first college English class I took, I discovered that I was a writer. I loved writing, rewriting, reading, proofreading, editing, changing and retyping; I did not stop until my heart sighed, happy with the final result. When my professor returned my first English paper, I had to look at the name twice to make sure it was mine. For the first time in my life, there on the upper right corner was a big, red A+! At the end of the essay, my professor had written, 'Camile, excellent work. You are a writer at heart. You should really consider English as your major.'

The Universe was not only sending me a sign, it was waving a banner in my face, trying to guide me towards my true path. As I recalled my first summer in college and the pride I had felt at excelling on my first English essay, I also remembered the times when I had sat in my grandparents' movie room and watched Hollywood classics, daydreaming of being a storyteller but thinking, 'I could never do that. I don't even live in the U.S. I can't even speak English.' But this time my mind quickly bounced back to the picture of that first A+ and the glorious feelings I had felt while I wrote that essay.

The Third Time the Voice Spoke

After coming back from my three-week vacation in Brazil, I lived a life of my daydreams coming true for approximately six months. I was divorced, independent and free to do what I wanted. In some ways, I began to let go and enjoy life to its fullest, the best way I knew how. I devoted myself to running, my job and my beloved bulldog, Lua. In my free time, I went out clubbing with girlfriends. Occasionally at work, when dealing with arrests, domestic disputes, child neglect calls or possession of drugs, I'd feel a little tugging inside my head, which I tried even harder to ignore it. It was the Voice again.

'Wrong place. Wrong life.'

I was too comfortable, however, to do anything about it. I worried about my bills, my retirement plan, terrified to have to start a brand new life all over again. My career became my identity. I was a runner and a police officer. I settled into that life and allowed it to take control of me. At the end of the six months ... I was still unfulfilled. I wanted more in every area of my life. I wanted to move into a different unit at work; I wanted to move into a different apartment; I wanted a relationship. I was desperately searching for something to fill the hole inside me. Nothing worked.

It was the Voice again. 'Wrong place. Wrong life.' I was too comfortable, however, to do anything about it.

One evening after running, I stopped by a friend's house to say a quick hello before going home and getting ready for the graveyard shift. We sat on her doorstep sipping our non-fat lattes and smoking cigarettes. We spoke about trivial things in our lives, when suddenly I felt as if someone had cupped their hands around my right ear and in a loud voice had said, 'It will all change.' I looked at my friend and told her, 'I feel my life is about to change. I don't know what will happen, but something will happen and it will bring huge changes with it.'

'Maybe the change will be something good! Something exciting!' she said, smiling at me. 'Maybe you'll meet someone or be transferred to a new unit at work.'

I smiled. 'Maybe.'

When I left for work, I didn't think twice about my sudden, short-lived revelation. I shut down every inlet and decided I would not pay attention to any of the signs the Universe had so kindly been trying to shove in my face. Instead, I dove head first into the craving for instant gratification, running myself harder, smoking more and shopping more. The only thing I knew was how to keep looking good and hiding the sad, confused person inside the impeccable body. I didn't know it, though, but the Universe was getting louder and speeding up, trying to find ways to make me pay attention.

Soon the Universe grew tired of soft whispers, loving interventions and subtle messages. I failed to see the divine order that is present in every moment. It takes some time to realise that everything that happens to us is for our own growth and benefit. Sometimes these lessons come disguised as 'good situations' and other times as 'bad situations.' The truth is that there is no good or bad. No happy, no sad. We label circumstances and states of mind according to our own flexibility to flow with the changes and accept that they are all there for a purpose. My stubbornness truly required a more aggressive approach from the Universe.

The only thing I knew was how to keep looking good and hiding the sad, confused person inside the impeccable body.

The Voice Shouts

Finally, on January 13, 2006, the Universe delivered the tough love I needed so much. It was a beautiful, warm Florida Friday. My squad member 'John' and I decided to attend the Art Deco Festival on South Beach after catching some hours of sleep after our graveyard shift. I slept for four hours and headed to South Beach to meet him and enjoy the festivities. Time flew by. Before we knew it, it was time to go back home and get ready for that night's shift. Shortly after roll call, John and I were dispatched to a domestic dispute. The call was dispatched in emergency mode; we quickly hopped into our separate police cars. With our sirens screaming and lights flashing, we headed towards the address given by the dispatcher. Upon arrival, only one party was on the scene, the female complainant. To my surprise, she was also Brazilian.

As I finished gathering the information from the complainant, John and I decided to go back to the station to fuel up our police vehicles. The lovely Florida Friday had turned into an evening rainstorm, intense and blinding. We took different routes. As I drove through the narrow streets of Miami Shores, the Universe's sound became louder. Just as I had been asleep in my life, I fell asleep at the wheel.

I remember the loud thump of my right rear tyre hitting the curb and making me lose control of my car on the rain-slicked streets. My car jumped the median and began heading towards a house in the neighbourhood. In those final seconds before impact, I desperately thought about the people sleeping inside, but unbeknownst to me, the house was empty. I quickly looked for something else to hit, and with seconds remaining I desperately steered the out-of-control car and pointed it as best as I could toward an old, thick ficus tree.

The impact was loud and brutal. It took my breath away, literally. Having battled asthma all my life, I thought I was having an asthma or panic attack from the shock of the impact. Later on in the hospital, they were to tell me that I had broken a total of nineteen ribs, twelve on my left side and one of them had punctured my left lung. Thinking to call for help, I tried to reach for my purse that had fallen to the passenger seat's floor, but I couldn't. Opening my door didn't work either. I was stuck.

I grabbed his hand, looked in his eye and said, 'Lieutenant, I can't feel my legs.'

Smoke poured from the engine and I became even more terrified. Would I burn alive? People streamed out of their houses, phones in their hands. Two tried to open my door and others called 911. I couldn't breathe, so I couldn't speak. In the distance, I heard the police radio and an officer's voice stating, 'Ma'am, we are here and there is no police vehicle accident.' I instantly knew they were talking about me. I reached for the mic, clicked it, took as deep a breath as I could, and after identifying myself to the police dispatcher I said, 'I can't breathe.' Long pause. 'I can't breathe ... I'm the one in the accident.' I gave the correct address. The dispatcher kept trying to get me back, but the pain was too great to speak anymore. John and Fire Rescue both arrived on the scene at the same time. I slipped in and out of consciousness while they extracted me from the police cruiser. As they rolled me away on the stretcher, I noticed that the scene was filled with officers from my district. My lieutenant accompanied me to the rescue truck and as they got ready to load me in I grabbed his hand, looked in his eye and said, 'Lt., I can't feel my legs.'

My life had finally changed.

Listening

When I woke up in the hospital after six weeks in an induced coma, the first thing I heard was the Voice. 'Many people are praying for you and cheering for you. You are not alone. You have never been alone. It will all be okay. You are exactly where you are supposed to be. This is your mission. Trust it. Accept it. Move forward. The love that surrounds you is immense and the energy is there. Believe it.'

I lay flat in my hospital bed. In my peripheral vision, I could see other beds to my side and around the room. About four or five nurses tended to the patients in that hospital unit I was in, which later I found out was the Trauma Intensive Care Unit. When one of the nurses, Gabriella, (I learned her name later), saw me awake, she smiled and said, 'Princess, you are our miracle girl. Look, everyone, Princess is awake.' Every nurse on duty came to my bedside and rejoiced in the fact I had my eyes open. I tried to speak but I couldn't, and when I tried, no sound came out. That is when I realised that I was hooked up to a ventilator that breathed for me. I no longer had control of my breathing. Every breath I took depended solely on a machine. I panicked a little, but the Voice I had heard earlier still echoed in my head, and I realised that I had no other choice but to trust it. The warnings had caught up to me, and now I was forced to let myself be guided by the Voice at last. I was forced, in that moment, to use the knowledge and wisdom it offered very graciously. I, at long, long last, had learned to listen.

The obstacles that followed the accident were unimaginable. Not only had I become a paraplegic at the thoracic level, but my body was still reconstructing itself after losing the function of my left lung, and days later, my right lung as well. I had broken a total of twenty-four bones. It was indeed a miracle that I had survived the six weeks in a coma. I grieved over the loss of my looks. I had become very skinny in the beginning and developed several stretch marks all over my body from the artificial weight gain corticosteroids caused. My once muscular strong legs atrophied to resembling little sticks. Chunks of my hair began to fall out and I cried, fearing it would never grow back. The stress made me break out. I was a mess. The Voice's powerful echo began to fade away as more health problems appeared. I longed to be alone to try to understand everything that was happening to me. I was constantly surrounded by family and friends who tried to give me the best support possible. I slipped into the darkest side of my soul. I felt betrayed by the Universe. I felt betrayed by the Voice. I felt like a failure.

During my five-month hospital stay, there was a constant struggle inside myself. I understood that my paralysis had been caused for a purpose; however, breaking the attachment from the physical side of the equation was extremely difficult. My life's messages became distant memories. I no longer heard whispers. Every chance I had to

I slowly began to understand the synchronicity of the messages in my life.

be alone, I would try to sort out my feelings about the tragedy that was happening to me, but also to try to receive feedback from the Universe; to hear the Voice again. I somehow knew I wasn't going to be abandoned at a moment like this. I sensed that everything I had gone through in life before my accident had prepared me for that moment. I needed guidance to continue on with my head held up high. I slowly began to understand the synchronicity of the messages in my life, even though they had stopped coming so loudly and so urgently.

After being moved to the in-patient rehabilitation unit of the hospital, and with less than one month left to be discharged, I developed tracheal stenosis, which is a common side-effect from long-term intubation. I was no longer ventilator-dependent, but had extreme difficulty in breathing. My windpipe had scar tissue that developed after they removed the ventilator and the first tracheotomy. I only had fifteen per cent of clear air space to get oxygen into my lungs. One Sunday afternoon, I had asked my mother to bring me some food from the hospital's food court. As she left the room, one of the assistant nurses came in to help me use the intermittent catheter. As we were finishing and she turned me on my side to clean me, I stopped breathing altogether.

The nursing staff resuscitated me. When I came to, I began to cry. I was enveloped by fear. Where was the Voice? Why was this happening to me? There were no answers, but something told me to keep listening.

I was discharged home with several medical issues, including my tracheal stenosis problem, unresolved. After my fifth trip back to the hospital to try to fix the tracheal stenosis, the doctors decided to give me a second tracheotomy. I lost my voice completely and breathed through a tube that stuck out of my throat. I mimicked words to communicate with my family and turned to food to drown the pain and the shame of what was happening to me. It wasn't long before the weight caught up with me. I didn't care any longer. I asked my step-dad to shave off my hair, hoping it would grow back thick and strong as it once had been. I cut off communication with the outside world. I was mad at the Universe for lying to me. I felt betrayed and alone. I didn't belong in this world anymore. And, worst of all, the Voice that I'd ignored for so long and had finally, helplessly, begun to trust, was gone. I drifted through the days, ignoring my friends' phone calls and emails, growing overly dependent on my immediate family, overcome with pain and self-pity.

Then, one night I had an amazing dream. I saw a bright light and felt warmth all over my body. The light spoke. 'You are not alone. I am always with you. Don't be scared. You are on the right path. Accept it. It is all up to you.' I understood. The tracheal stenosis wasn't a betrayal or a bad practical joke played by divine beings. It was a reminder. 'Stop caring only about how you look. Look inside and care for the person inside the body too.' For a little over four months, I did not speak and only breathed through the tube in my throat. As this missing piece of the puzzle fit itself into my heart and head, I began to take charge of my health and future.

In September 2006, I flew to Brazil to have tracheal surgery there and fix my tracheal stenosis problem completely. It was there that I heard, 'Write a book,' for the first time. I knew then that I wasn't ready for the task, but when the time would come to begin writing I would know; I would be told. After spending a year and a half there, taking care of my health, rediscovering and re-creating myself, listening to my dear guiding Voice and planning for the endless possibilities that lay ahead for me in my new life, I finally came back to the United States.

As I continued on my physical, emotional and spiritual journey, signs began to manifest around me more frequently. I was finally able to hear the Voice again. My listening skills were deeply heightened, but I didn't continue to just idly sit and listen; I had questions that I asked often and expected answers.

I reflected often on the old life I had lived, still missing feeling beautiful and independent and craving the endorphins that running had provided me. I sat in my chair, day in and day out. Sometimes I lay in bed all day and turned inward to a world I never dared explore before. At first, right at the beginning of this journey, I had thought the Universe was being too perverse. I couldn't see the divine order being played out. There was no way I could deal with everything I was being dealt; I lacked the self-confidence and some of the will to fight. I didn't have the wisdom then that I have now, that nothing is by chance. But, now I can see it as clearly as I can hear my own voice.

Nothing is Wasted

Churning beneath my reflections at that time there was still an unrelenting fear, a fear that often dominated my thoughts. Will I be able to adjust to life in a wheelchair? Will I succeed? Will I matter? Will I be loved? But, with the help of my guiding voice and the unconditional love of friends and family, I began to see the bright light inside myself shining through the body sitting in the wheelchair. Slowly, I began to know me. It was exhilarating to find out that I was an extraordinary person after all. It was mind boggling that I even thought of myself as extraordinary because as much as I knew that I was a remarkable human being, I feared the discrimination of being different. I still held some self-worth attachments to the way I looked.

After returning home, I spent two years in physical therapy to regain my strength and learn to adapt to my new life. Although I now had a sense of urgency to do things that I felt I had to do, the Voice reminded me, ' All in its due time.' I began to drive again and regained ninety per cent of my independence that way. I learned that although looks are not everything, taking care of our bodies helps our minds and souls. They are all connected, and the equilibrium that one brings to the other is paramount to optimal health. For the first time in over thirty years, I began to love myself. I loved myself for everything I had gone through, all the visible scars on my body, all the tears I had shed, for the hard moments I endured.

I was grateful for it all.

There was no more shame.

There is no more shame.

I love me for who I once was, who I am and for the person I aim to be.

I never believed in my own strength until I was put through my own tests. Some people tell me that, maybe, I should have been careful with what I had wished for because I had been so bored with life and its mundaneness. In response to them, I say that going through my accident and becoming paralysed have been immense blessings. Not only have I gotten to

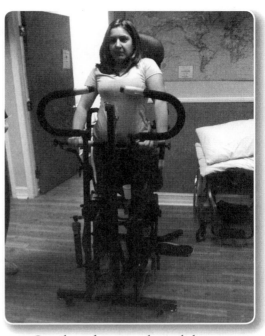

Camile undergoing physical therapy

know the beautiful soul inside this vessel, but also I have met and connected with other amazing beings that I would not have had the pleasure to meet if I were not in a wheelchair. I opened up to life. In return, life opened up to me. I now hear and see life's signs all the time.

These signs are all around, all the time, for all of us. We are often so caught up in our own self-pity party that we forget to connect with the person who is smiling at us in line at Starbucks or to appreciate the gift of taking a deep breath while sitting in gridlock traffic. We fail to live in the present and smell the flowers, watch a beautiful sunset or enjoy the smell of the ocean. We don't get to know the stranger that sits inside our own body and to listen.

Every time we stop listening to our gut feeling, we become strangers to ourselves. We dishonour our authentic nature. Listening and paying attention are not hard to do. Stop for a couple of minutes a day. Go somewhere inspiring if you can, or close your eyes and imagine yourself there. Take deep breaths in and out until you can feel yourself relax and think only about your breathing. Your brain will subside and a voice will arise. Listen. Do not analyse it. Listen, lovingly. Do not judge it. You are not crazy. The Voice exists. It exists because you are here. It is here to guide you, to love you. Accept its truth and you will find yourself more at ease with life and what it is you are here to fulfil. This Voice will take you there; as mine did.

My blessed experiences since I first hit that ficus tree have taught me to live a life worth living. Above all I have learned to love myself and honour the desire to be kind to me, even when the old habit of self-criticising, or the tiny fear of not being accepted creeps up on me. I am worthy. I no longer run. I no longer run towards anything or from anything. I sit, breathe and listen. Although I have lost control of over two-thirds of my physical body, I feel as if I had gained control of an entire parallel Universe.

I am finally writing. When I write, I feel connected with every living micro-organism in the Universe. I feel present and alive. I am invited to speak at seminars and workshops. At first, I would be terrified of talking about myself for the whole time. After my first couple of times, however, I understood the immense gift life was presenting to me by allowing me to share my story and inspire others to listen to their own voice and to not wait for the Universe to intervene in a more 'in-your-face' way.

When things seem out of control, when you feel lost and unimportant, make a list of what is valuable to you in your life; be unbiased and unprejudiced. Whatever you write as your number one priority is where your passion lays. Whether it is scrap-booking, writing, reading, watching movies, children, family, pets or plants, it does not matter what your first priority is. It is yours and yours only to do something about. Talk to your guiding voice to implement that passion in your everyday life. That will help you take your life to the next level and you will be fulfilled in what you do. This might take time or it may happen within a day. The important thing is that you listen to yourself and don't deny the true nature of who you are.

Once you start seeing results, pass this secret forward. Breathe deeply. Live your own life. Be grateful. The voice within is sacred.

Suggestions to Help You Live Extraordinarily by Listening to Your Own Voice Within

 Take the time to breathe deeply

Allow yourself to relax and breathe. Breathing deeply in and out increases brain capacity. It is also an instant relaxation technique. When both are combined, your body will automatically go from sympathetic mode to para-sympathetic mode and will function more wisely. Once we follow the natural rhythms of our bodies through our breath, brain noise will subside and you may hear a quiet 'Hello'. This is your inner wisdom introducing itself to you and hoping you will take the time to listen to its loving guidance.

Create a special place

It is of equal importance for our surroundings to be congruent with whom we are. If you would like to delve deeper into the world of inner wisdom, creating or relocating yourself to a sacred space will give you the confidence you need and boost your receptive senses to what your intuition has to offer. You may like to walk on the beach while watching a magnificent sunrise or sunset. You may rather sit in a garden, taking in the aroma of different flowers. It might suit you better to see the world from the top of a mountain; different perspectives stimulate open-mindedness. Or you might be comfortable in the cosiness of your own home, in a special room that you have created as your own getaway. And, when all else fails, you always have your own imagination. Sit quietly and imagine yourself wherever you'd like to be; shortly you will be there and your voice of wisdom will soon manifest itself.

Listen carefully and take action

Your gut knows. It is paramount that you do not judge what you hear. You always have free will to do what you choose; however, you know when your gut speaks to you. That is the feeling you will have when you hear something important from the little voice that knows. If you don't act upon it, you will have that nagging feeling all day long reminding you, 'What if?'

So, be brave, get out of the comfort zone and try what it feels like to listen and trust yourself once in a while. The benefits are immeasurable.

GET YOUR EXTRAORDINARY
FREE GIFT BONUS

Camile Araujo is kindly offering a **FREE BONUS GIFT** to all readers of this book.

The Voice Within: A Guide to Unveil the Melodic Sounds of Your Soul

An eWorkbook that presents exercises and inspirational quotes that heighten your listening habits and inspire you to follow your voice of wisdom.

Simply visit the web page below and follow the directions to directly download *The Voice Within.*

www.camilearaujo.com

'Heart Living is living in balance;
instead of focusing on a left-brain oriented way
of looking at the world, life centres in the
feeling, knowing heart ...'

Cynthia Zeki Ph.D.

Cynthia Zeki Ph.D. is a gifted heart-based energy healer, teacher, speaker, author and radio host who lives and works in the energy of the heart. Based in Chicago, Illinois, USA, she loves to help others discover the gentle joy, deep peace and profound love in Heart Living through retreats, individual consultations and her monthly internet radio show, *Wake Up Sunshine*, on I am Healthy Radio. Dr. Cynthia teaches people how to use the power of Divine Love to reunite left-brain thinking and right-brain creativity with heart wisdom, for truer, deeper spiritual and personal understanding.

Dr. Cynthia's heart wisdom has been given to her by Divine Love Guidance through intensive meditation, self-healing and other energy work. As a healer working in Heart Energy, she channels archangels and is a medium for loved ones and guides so that each beautiful soul who comes to her can open their hearts and live life fully in their own Divine Love. Dr. Cynthia is a Reiki Master Teacher and practices and teaches classes in Akashic Record Reading, Reiki Crystal Healing and the Violet Ray Tradition. She has taught throughout Asia and the USA. As an active member of Edgar Cayce's Association for Research and Enlightenment (A.R.E.), Dr. Cynthia teaches classes and gives healings at the Heartland A.R.E and other locations in the Chicago area. She is a former board member of Unity in Lincoln Park and is guided by Unity's teaching of positive spirituality in her work.

Dr. Cynthia has a wonderful relationship with her unbelievably intelligent and gorgeous daughter, Jasmine. After opening her own heart, Dr. Cynthia was divinely led to Thomas, the absolute love of her life, who fully supports and engages in Heart Living with her. They live a blessed and loving life together and with Una, their one-eyed cat.

Heart Living

CYNTHIA ZEKI Ph.D.

I've always been a thinker. I lived a good portion of my life as an academic. I went from my BA straight to my MA in linguistics and then taught English as a Second Language in colleges in China, Taiwan and in the United States. When I wasn't sure if my marriage was going to last, I decided to move my one-year-old daughter and myself from Florida to Ohio to pursue my Ph.D. This decision wasn't based on a love of learning (although I do have that) or a desire to be called 'Doctor', but simply because I was good at school and knew that no matter what happened with my marriage, as a professor I would be able to support my child.

Although I was very successful in my professional life – after I graduated I was given an assistant professor position in Chicago, beating over one hundred other applicants – my personal life was always a mess. My first marriage failed and I dated one train wreck after another until I married the biggest train wreck of them all. Most of my female friends were needy and bitter, and it seemed like I was always soothing this one or pacifying that one. There was little give and take in any of my relationships, just a lot of me giving and them taking. I was often sick and always exhausted and unhappy.

During one particularly trying time in my life, I picked up the Dalai Lama's book, *The Art of Happiness.* Hmmm, I thought, Happiness as art, something you create. The title alone intrigued me. I found a lot of solace in that book and began to practice meditation and mindfulness. I left academia and became a massage therapist because it required presence and mindfulness. Giving a massage was meditative for me, and soon enough I had a thriving practice.

While for the first time in my life I knew peace and happiness, it was far from a constant state of being. Practicing this life seemed almost like being on a diet – when life was easy and uneventful, I could easily stay in the groove. But after a nasty fight with my then-husband or disappointment in a friend, I would fall off the wagon; my meditation would stop, my mindfulness would stop, I would revert back to those miserable thought patterns of unhappiness. I lived this cycle for many years.

After my second marriage finally expired, I was in so much pain and anguish that my heart finally got my attention. I was at the point when I couldn't even be mad at my ex-husband. In reality, he had showed me his true colours from the beginning, and I had used every trick my brain offered me to stay involved – I rationalised, I explained, I excused, I ignored, I denied. And after all of that, I realised my whole life had been focused mostly in my left-brain thought – the rational brain. The meditation practice was a nice right-brain distraction, but every time my usual reality reared its ugly head I ping-ponged back to my left-brain thought patterns and habits.

I was far from alone in this. Most of us live in a left-brain world. Left-brain thought is using all the information that we've been told and/or believed about ourselves and all the experiences we've had or witnessed in the past before we move forward; it's what is often termed 'ego'. While we certainly need our left-brain thought to live a full human life, being primarily in the left brain inhibits growth and understanding on all levels. By definition, left-brain thought is restrictive because we tend to think and do only that which we know or believe makes sense.

Left-brain thought is restrictive because we tend to think and do only that which we know or believe makes sense.

Meanwhile, my poor heart kept getting more and more closed and more and more blocked. It was pretty easy to dismiss it – after all, feelings aren't rational, not scientific, not quantifiable, not even reasonable. However, the searing pain and anguish were relentless; it was my heart gasping for air. Finally, the only release I could give it was to cry.

I had never been much of a crier – crying was for sissies and weaklings, and I was neither. But now I cried, almost constantly it seemed, and for no apparent reason. I cried for almost six months straight. I would cry in the car on the way to work and again on the way home. I'd cry when I was giving a massage if the music I was listening to hit my heart. I cried watching TV. I cried fixing dinner. I cried when I went for my morning walk. My daughter thought I was nuts, and I did, too. But I did not even try to stop that flow of tears.

Surprisingly enough, the tears weren't tears of sadness or even of joy. They were cleansing tears, and each one popped open a link in the chain that was keeping my heart locked up and closed. And when the crying was finally (mostly) done, I was amazed to find what a wise, beautiful space my heart was.

One of my favourite spiritual teachers, Pema Chodron, describes the heart this way:

> 'When you begin to touch your heart or let your heart be touched,
> you begin to discover that it's bottomless, that it doesn't have any
> resolution, that this heart is huge, vast and limitless.
> You begin to discover how much warmth and gentleness is there,
> as well as how much space.'

I spent the next several years listening to and focusing on my heart. I discovered that in my heart I am perfect just as I am. I realised that my body is just the housing of the true essence and beauty of who I am. I found wisdom and truth and trust and all kinds of wonderful qualities that I had paid lip service to but had never really felt because feelings are the heart's domain, not the brain's.

I discovered the spark of Divine Love within my heart that was my soul's true connection to Spirit. And because that love was divine, it was absolutely unconditional. I found true love and acceptance of myself in my heart and that because the love in my heart was also divine it too was limitless; there was plenty of love and acceptance for everyone else. With the infinite love from Spirit in and through my heart, I found there was no need for judgment, negativity or any other limiting ideas.

I found the peace and beauty of Heart Living. Simply put, Heart Living is living in balance; instead of focusing on a left-brain oriented way of looking at the world, life centres in the feeling, knowing heart and goes from there to the thinking left brain and creating right brain.

While a lot of the self-help and/or spiritual growth writings bash the ego, when left-brain thought is balanced with right-brain creativity and knowing from the heart, ego is actually not a bad thing. It allows us to use the vast knowledge we've acquired throughout our lives in a way that is truly our own. When it's the only way of living, however, it leads to being judgmental and critical of oneself and others, fearful of trying and exploring new ideas, and keeps one stuck in a rut. It can also be very frustrating because we are constantly looking for answers, and a lot of life cannot be explained. This can lead to bitterness and clinging onto emotions and thoughts that no longer serve us.

The right brain is an important counter-balance to the left brain. It is where creativity, imagination and intuition come into play. Thinking of a beautiful picture in your mind immediately pulls you out of your chattering left brain and opens the channel to your heart. It also can help you come up with new ideas and fresh ways of looking at the world.

As a spiritual being or soul having a human experience, you were born with choice.

So, why should you try Heart Living? Why not just focus on your right brain and follow your intuition and your imagination? Basically, your intuition and imagination are tools. As a spiritual being or soul having a human experience, you were born with choice. Following intuition and/or imagination without heart wisdom makes you a puppet and can lead to separation from the human experience and even from your fellow humans.

For example, I went to dinner with two very good friends, 'Alice' and 'Fred'. Alice had brought along a friend of hers, 'Maria'. Alice had told me that Maria was very intuitively gifted and she was eager for us to meet. I enjoyed Maria's company; she was lively and fun. During dinner, Fred was talking in glowing terms about his daughter. Maria asked Fred if she was his only child. Fred smiled in discomfort, but Maria was insistent. Finally, Fred admitted that he had another child with whom he had little contact. Maria affirmed that she had thought so.

Maria was using the intuition she received through her right brain without bringing that information into her heart. Had she done so, she might have realised that Fred had shared the information he had wanted to share and it was rude and thoughtless of her to push him to disclose what was very personal to him. This would have saved everyone from an evening of awkwardness.

Indeed, the true essence of who you are is in your heart. This is where your wisdom, joy, beauty – all the magnificence that you are – resides. When you live from your heart first, you are living the life that you are truly meant to. And because you know this, your discernment and compassion grow exponentially, and all judgment is more easily released; your heart is where pure, divine love for you and for all resides.

Are you still having doubts? Try this quick exercise. Let's say 'Read this book'. Now after each of the phrases say the phrase 'Read this book'.

1. I think I should _____.

2. From what I've learned, it seems like a good idea to _____.

3. I dreamt last night that I should _____.

4. I woke up this morning with the idea to _____.

5. I feel in my heart that I should _____.

6. I know in my heart that I should _____.

Now, out of (1) – (6), which feels most powerful to you? (1) & (2) are left-brain thought. (3) & (4) are right-brain intuition and imagination. (5) & (6) are heart feelings. If you chose (5) or (6), you understand the power of Heart Living.

If you need another example to help grasp this further, as an extra exercise you could think back to a decision you have recently made and insert it in each statement (1) to (6) and say them aloud. Then you can assess whether your decision had been left-brain-, right-brain- or heart-centred.

Feeling – Vibration and Resonance

Heart Living understands that your own truth, the very centre of who you are and what is right for you, is neither a thought nor an idea but a feeling. In this case, a feeling does not refer to an emotional response; it's a resonance and/or a vibration that is experienced in the heart. Most of us have been taught and trained to think in a certain way and to have a specific reaction to a specific situation. We call this reaction a feeling, but it's actually an emotional response that is the result of left-brain conditioning.

Let's look at this example. Let's say your spouse comes home and tells you he/she is going to marry someone else. What is your response? Do you scream in anger? Do you break down in tears, thinking you didn't even see this divorce coming? Or do you jump for joy, thinking you finally have a way to escape?

Now think of what your response would be if you lived in a polygamous society, such as on the TV shows *Sister Wives* or *Big Love*. Or what your response would be if you lived in a rural society where the women (or men) do the hard, back-breaking work and each family functions separately?

Heart Living understands that your own truth, the very centre of who you are and what is right for you, is neither a thought nor an idea but a feeling.

Depending on which situation you are in, you would probably have a different emotional response, conditioned by your family's beliefs, the society in which you live and the experiences you have had. If in a polygamous society, you might welcome the new friendship, while in the rural setting you might welcome the extra help. In modern society, you might be devastated (or very angry). In any case, your emotional response would most likely differ to the one that was triggered when the question was first asked. Often we jump straight to conditioned, emotional response and don't stop and listen to what the heart has communicated first. Our heart communication tells us to first stop and look at our own beliefs and values, and to determine what our responsibility in the matter is, what is our lesson and what action can be taken that is for our highest good.

So, in modern society, if your spouse wanted to marry another person, your heart would help you determine if this is truly in your highest good. Your heart helps you go underneath the surprise, anger or devastation that is triggered by your emotional response. You might discover that you have not appreciated your spouse and have been so caught up with your own problems that you have ignored his or hers. You might discover that you are expecting your spouse to bring you happiness and joy instead of finding it for yourself. Or you might discover that you two have truly led separate lives for a long time and it is a blessing to end the marriage.

Once you know your own responsibility in the situation, you can look at your own beliefs and values. Do you believe that marriage is 'until death do you part'? If so, the lesson for you may be to honour your marriage by consciously taking time every day expressing love and gratitude to your spouse. Because you truly value the institution of marriage, you will take every action available, such as going to counselling, to improve your marriage. This is in your highest good.

Heart Living is giving our first and foremost attention to vibration and resonance and then using that information with our left-brain thought and right-brain creativity.

On the other hand, if you believe that you have stayed in the marriage out of habit and convenience, or fear of change, you will realise it truly is in your highest good to end the marriage. Your heart can help you remember the good in the experience and release the bad. You can then take the necessary steps coming from that heart place of neutrality instead of anger and have a smooth transition.

Our heart communicates through those very feelings of vibration and resonance that I mentioned. Heart Living is giving our first and foremost attention to vibration and resonance and then using that information with our left-brain thought and right-brain creativity.

A vibration is the level at which your energy and the energy of all things resides. All vibrations are energy, and energy is not static. Because of this, any vibration, including your own, changes. The good thing is with practice you can keep yourself at a higher vibration. A high vibration is associated with good feelings such as peace, love and happiness. Lower vibrations don't feel so good and are associated with worry, lack, fear, and so on.

As an example, think of something that's bugging you right now. Are you worried about your financial situation? Did a friend or loved one irritate you? Hold on to that fear, worry or irritation and focus on how it feels. Do you feel like you are able to move forward easily with confidence or do you feel bogged down? Does your heart feel light or heavy? Do you feel hopeful or hopeless? If you feel this heaviness and restriction, you are vibrating at a lower level.

Now take a couple of deep breaths. See this same picture in your mind with a positive outcome. You have made up with whoever has irritated you, your worries have been resolved and all is well. You are abundant and prosperous and at peace, as are all your loved ones. At this moment in time you feel immensely grateful.

Now how does that feel? Does your heart feel more open, and do you feel like you are soaring? Do you feel like you can embrace the world? Most likely you feel freedom and expansiveness, and this is because you are vibrating at a higher level. When you live from your heart, you naturally vibrate at a higher level.

While vibration is what you feel for yourself, resonance is when you get a strong feeling about someone or something else. This feeling is in your heart and body, and not just your head. Resonance is a feeling that touches your heart and makes you pay attention. A wonderful resonance is a match to your vibration or a slightly higher vibration than yours at a particular time. A discordant resonance is one that is either much lower or much higher than your vibration. A wonderful resonance acts as confirmation while a discordant resonance is an opportunity for growth and understanding.

If you have a friend that you don't see very often but when you do it's like you've never been apart, that's a wonderful resonance. If you meet someone for the first time and it feels like you've known them forever, that's a wonderful resonance. If you go someplace and you breathe deeply and it feels like home to you, that's a wonderful resonance.

Sometimes resonance can feel like a jolt. This is a discordant resonance and often hits us strongly, sometimes as aversion, anger or distaste. We immediately want to judge or even attack the person who triggers that reaction in us. While it's common for us to focus on the other person or situation, it is truly our own heart telling us, 'Uh oh, I need to pay attention to this.' This kind of resonance gives us a great chance to look at our own beliefs and assumptions. While disconcerting, it's always an opportunity for learning and growth, especially if we focus on our own feelings and not the outside source. It's a grand occasion for us to open our heart even more.

Once I was out enjoying a cocktail with another good friend, 'Donna'. Donna is a very successful businesswoman, very smart and creative, and a beautiful soul. An older woman came in the restaurant wearing a very tight micro-mini dress. She had lots of bright blue eye shadow, rose red cheeks and fire engine red lips. Her grey hair was pulled into a high ponytail. I smiled when I saw her; she was such a contrast to everyone else and I idly wondered about her life's story.

It's always an opportunity for learning and growth, especially if we focus on our own feelings and not the outside source.

Donna, on the other hand, went ballistic. She angrily mocked the woman, and when the woman left the room, Donna even got up to follow her. She then called her sleeping husband to try to get him to join us to see this woman. It took every ounce of cajoling and convincing I could muster to get Donna to leave the restaurant and go on home. I was stunned at the strength and ferocity of her reaction – after all, she didn't even know the woman!

The next day, Donna and I talked. I asked her what it was about the woman that had upset her so. She said that she was too old and ugly to dress like that and her make-up made her look like some sort of pathetic clown. I let Donna ramble on about the woman until she had nothing else to say about her.

Then I gently asked Donna, 'What does that woman's appearance or actions have to do with you? She didn't dress in that manner to infuriate you – she doesn't even know you.'

Donna sat for a moment, feeling stunned herself. She was so focused on this woman she hadn't bothered to ask herself why she reacted so strongly. Then she slowly explained that maybe it was because her marriage wasn't working out and she was afraid of what her future held. She didn't want to end up like that. This realisation hit her like a tonne of bricks.

Donna's experience was a discordant resonance where two very different levels of vibration come into contact with each other. Therefore, she had immediately reacted externally and with much more intensity than the situation called for. When she was able to turn her focus to herself, she was able to uncover her own fears and receive the gift from the experience. It was a good time to look at, address and resolve her fears.

An example of a discordant, higher vibrational resonance happened with me about a year ago. I met a woman, Barbara, who just radiated peace and love and Spirit. She was an older woman, full of elegance, beauty and grace. Barbara runs a non-profit organisation dedicated to giving young people training in eco-friendly jobs so that they can feel a sense of passion and purpose. Her studio and classrooms are filled with fascinating equipment and beautiful treasures from the earth. I felt truly blessed to be able to teach a class there. When Barbara smiled, I felt like God had covered me with a warm blanket. When she talked to me, I felt like a blushing, giggly schoolgirl, not like a woman of the same standing – I went into child-mode and actually felt some nerves.

Barbara invited me to teach a class again this year, and I gratefully accepted. I got to spend a lot more time with her and our friendship deepened greatly. While I was still very honoured to be in her presence, I also felt a lot more comfortable. I realised that through my own spiritual practice over the past year we were now more of a vibrational match and thus had a wonderful resonance with each other. We could truly enjoy each other's company much more now.

Resonance and vibrations are feelings, and using your feelings to guide you in every part of your life is the foundation of Heart Living. Albert Einstein knew the power of feelings when he said, 'I believe in intuitions and inspirations ... I sometimes feel that I am right. I do not know that I am.' And look at what unique contributions Einstein made to the world by believing so!

Resonating with Beauty

Heart Living encourages your heart to open and blossom, and it helps you to understand your deepest truths. You are then free to live in this truth and share it with others. Living in and sharing your heart's truth gives you the deep peace, radiant love and constant happiness that is Heart Living. A delightful way to start practising Heart Living is by noticing and appreciating beauty.

When I see beauty, a smile starts in my heart and works its way up to my face; beauty is such a powerful resonance that it makes me stop, catch my breath and experience awe, wonder and gratitude, all at the same time. Beauty can touch each of us at our very heart core.

A delightful way to start practising Heart Living is by noticing and appreciating beauty.

One of my strongest memories of the power of beauty happened way back in 1983 when I was living in China, teaching English at the Sichuan Foreign Language Institute in Chongqing, Sichuan Province. I was fresh out of college and had never been out of the U.S. China was incredibly different from anything I had experienced before. While it was definitely a challenging time, I also learned a lot and enjoyed the various experiences immensely.

In the early eighties, China was one big mass of grey. The people were still wearing what basically was the Mao suit – formless, faded cotton pants and jackets in dark blue, olive green or a nondescript grey. Sichuan in general did not get a lot of sun, and whatever it did get was obscured by a thick haze of coal smoke and dust. Chongqing was a hilly, industrial town with lots of people and pollution but not a whole lot of ancient history or culture. So, when I had the chance, I travelled to Chengdu, the capital of Sichuan. Chengdu had a history of over 2,000 years, with beautiful temples and tea houses and streets to wander in. I would set out from the hotel in the morning, armed with a map and a Chinese-English dictionary, and just stroll along. I loved spending weekends like this and always had interesting adventures.

One grey afternoon, I was poking around an old neighbourhood, browsing in tiny shops as I looked for a jade inkwell or other souvenirs. I came out of a dimly-lit store, turned a corner and stopped in my tracks. There in front of me was one of the most beautiful and amazing sights I had ever seen.

It was a woman dressed in a costume so ornate I thought she must be a performer in a Chinese opera. Her dress was long and white with full sleeves and a high neck. Every opening and seam was trimmed with a border of bright, multi-coloured ribbon. She had a long, bright pink apron tied at her waist. Her long, jet-black hair was carefully styled with streams of ribbons for decorations. She was wearing several ornate, silver necklaces with turquoise and enamelled pendants. Her boots were finely and colourfully embroidered, with toes that curled up at the end.

The beauty of a Tibetan woman

There could not have been a bigger contrast to the rest of the population and the general colour of the landscape. I stared and stared, drinking it all in. Her ruddy pink complexion. Her liquid black eyes.

And then I realised I had brought her to a standstill as well. My light curly hair. My green eyes and light skin. My height, my shape, my blue jeans, red boots and colourful purse. At exactly the same time, we began to smile. We smiled until we were beaming at each other, and then we both nodded our heads in acknowledgement and respect. She turned back around and walked away.

I stood a while longer, basking in the lingering light of her beauty, savouring the memory of the colours and the gleam in her eyes. I felt warm all over. I learned later that she was Tibetan; Chengdu was the gateway to Tibet at the time. When I asked my Chinese colleagues about her, they did not share my fascination. But for me, the gentle warmth of that woman's smile and the beauty of her clothing and spirit have stayed in my heart for almost thirty years. I am sure that the warmth and beauty that still resonates in my heart when I recall her helped trigger my interest in the Dalai Lama and my study of Tibetan Buddhism that continues to this day.

I stood a while longer, basking in the lingering light of her beauty, savouring the memory of the colours and the gleam in her eyes.

As you can see, beauty as a personal resonance in your heart is different from what is thought to be beautiful. When we think of beauty we use our left brain. We think, 'Wow! That supermodel is beautiful! Look at her long limbs, her big blue eyes, her flowing blonde hair.' Or we will analyse a piece of art or music based on its style, composition or merit. But just because you think something is beautiful does not necessarily mean it resonates with your heart. I can certainly appreciate the beauty of a Renoir painting, but none of his work resonates in my heart like Monet's does. When I visited the D'Orsay Museum in Paris, I slowly walked by and admired the Renoir paintings; I stopped and inhaled and felt the Monet paintings. They absolutely exhilarated me.

When your heart is open to feel beauty's resonance, you are naturally more present, aware and positive in your daily life. Appreciation of beauty's resonance is an important part of Heart Living.

When someone walks into our home for the first time, they almost always comment how peaceful and cosy it is. This is not by accident – I have purposely created my home to be a sanctuary where only things that resonate in my heart are displayed. Of course, I have family photos but not a lot at one time, just the ones that resonate. I have some art from China and from other places that I have travelled to. We have some crystals and shells and other wonders of nature. Some of Thomas' collections of African masks are in the hall and his lovely Himalayan singing bowls are on the mantle. Everything we see resonates in our heart, and if it no longer does, we remove it. Our home is not cluttered or filled with meaningless objects. Therefore, it is and feels beautiful to us.

While my entire home feels beautiful to me, I also have a sacred space dedicated to my Heart Living practice. Having a dedicated space allows you to sub-consciously calm down and centre in your heart before you even begin your heart practice or meditation. This space can be a room or a quiet corner or even just a chair; what is most important is that this place is quiet, comfortable and beautiful to you.

Sacred Space – Connecting With Your Heartspace

The resonance of beauty can involve any or all of the senses, so be open to using them all as you collect objects for your sacred space. Walk around your house and collect objects that resonate with you visually. Is there a beautiful photograph of a loved one and/or a treasured souvenir from a special place or event in your life? Do you have any special crystals, shells or plants? Put them all aside for your sacred space. Do you have a favourite scented candle or incense? Use that for your sacred space as well. Do you have a soft pillow and/or blanket that are inviting to the touch? They, too, belong in your sacred space.

How about a portable CD or MP3 player? Having quiet, meditative music or sounds of nature can help you to be in your heartspace more easily. Be sure there is a small table for a glass of water or a cup of tea or coffee, even a small healthy snack. You want your sacred space to be so beautiful and complete that you don't want to leave it!

If space is at a premium in your home and you can't have a dedicated space available all the time, put all the objects for your sacred space in a box so you can put them out when you want to, but are out of the way for the other parts of your day.

When you are engaged in Heart Living, you have constant connection to the wisdom in your heart. Heart wisdom is different from knowledge; knowledge is the information we've acquired through formal and informal education and our life experiences. We access our knowledge mostly through our left brain. Wisdom is the deeper knowing, the bigger picture, that helps awaken the truth in our soul.

We become familiar with our heart wisdom through intuition and resonance. Because you picked objects for your sacred space by feeling their resonance, each object is a key to the wisdom in your heart. The following Heart Living practice will help you to access this wisdom.

Sit in your sacred space with your beautiful objects around you within easy reach. You will also need a notebook or journal and a pen to write with. First, you will practice a visualisation that takes you down into your heartspace. You will then take your beautiful objects into that space with you, hold them and intuitively receive any information or wisdom they have to share. You will then let this information flow from your heart to your hand and onto your journal.

Sacred Object Heartspace Wisdom Practice

1.   In your mind's eye, 'see' (visualise) in front of you a series of seven steps. Climb up each step.

2.   At the top of the stairs, look out at a lovely scene in nature.

3.   Add some beautiful trees, plants and flowers to your scene.

4.   Add some friendly animals and birds if you'd like to.

5.   Make sure the sky is perfect and the temperature is comfortable.

6.   In the middle of your scene, add a place for you to sit and rest.

7.   Go over to this seat, make yourself comfortable and relax. This is your safe and happy spot.

8.   When you are ready, rise from your seat and return to the top of the stairs.

9.   Go back down the seven steps and find yourself on a platform. Coming up the platform is a beam of spiralling yellow gold light.

10.   Sense this platform is just above your nose, inside the top nasal passages. See or feel yourself sliding down this beam as it spirals down, down, down behind your nose, behind your throat, until it just reaches to the inside of your ribcage.

11.   Feel or see the deep energy of this place, and continue down the

spiralling beams as it goes behind your lungs and ends at your heart. This is your heartspace. See or feel a warm, comforting space where there is nothing but Divine Love, Truth and Clarity.

12. Now bring your awareness to the beautiful objects you have around you in your sacred space. Reach out and take one and hold it gently in your hands.

13. Now close your eyes and gently ask if this object can help provide any wisdom or understanding for you.

14. Gently put the object back down and open your eyes.

15. Now freely and easily write whatever information comes to you. Don't think about it; just start writing.

16. Repeat Steps 12 through 15 for all the objects in your sacred space.

17. After you have put the last object back and finished your writing, continue to breathe deeply and fully. When you are ready to leave your heartspace, see or feel yourself rise back up the beam of light until you're back on the platform.

18. Climb back up the seven steps and rest in the seat in your safe and happy spot.

19. Take a couple of deep breaths, and then go back over to the top of the stairs.

20. Turn around and express gratitude to your safe and happy spot.

21. Go back down the seven steps.

22. Take a deep breath or two and open your eyes.

This practice can lead to true insight into what is within your heart. When my daughter first went away to college and I missed her companionship, I often sat in my heartspace with a Mother's Day card she had made for me. I easily felt the love, joy and appreciation she had felt when she made it, and this invariably brightened my day.

When my father was ill before he passed away, he, my mother, my daughter and I all made a trip to the Florida State Fair. We had a truly lovely day and he bought a brown agate slice as a souvenir. After he died, I went into his bedroom and I could almost feel that stone calling me. I took it home and I sit with it often in my heartspace. In that stone I feel the power of my father's love and his unfailing support and interest in my business and my life. It is a source of great solace.

The more time you spend in your sacred space with your special objects, the more familiar your heartspace will become. Knowing what your heart wisdom feels like, and following the insights and intuition you receive there, will help you easily and consistently experience the deep peace, profound love and gentle joy that is Heart Living.

Heart Living helped me find the true love of my life in my husband, Thomas. Our relationship is filled with deep caring, joy, compassion and true friendship since we both communicate from a point of the Divine Love in our hearts. I love friends and family alike for who they are, and they love me the same way. Because I love myself, I put my health first – I eat good food, rest and sleep well, and I do activities I enjoy, like riding my bike or going for a nice walk. I have no stress-related illnesses such as high blood pressure or migraines.

Through Heart Living I am kind, gentle and loving to myself and with all. I naturally focus on the good and the positive in every part of my life and give little time, energy or thought to anything or anyone that does not resonate with the loving truth in my heart. And this has allowed me to live a fuller, happier, more loving and more peaceful life than I ever imagined possible. I hope that you too can enjoy the bliss of Heart Living.

Suggestions to Help You Live Extraordinarily Through the Love and Joy of Heart Living

Open and close each part of your day with heartfelt appreciation

Open and close each part of your day with heartfelt appreciation by placing your hands on your heart and saying words of gratitude. At the beginning of each day, say 'Thank you for a new and glorious day.' At the end of the day, 'Thank you for this glorious day I just experienced.' When you arrive at work, say 'Thank you for this job and the opportunities it provides for me.' When you leave work say, 'Thank you for this job and another successful day. This part of my day is now over and done.' When you prepare and eat your dinner, say 'Thank you for the opportunity to prepare and eat this delicious and nourishing meal.' And when you are finished say, 'Thank you for the lovely meal. Dinner is now done and I embrace the relaxation and rest of this evening.' Opening and closing each part of your day discourages left-brain rumination and encourages peaceful Heart Living.

Tune into your body and your feelings

Carry a small and beautiful object such as a lovely crystal with you. Pause throughout your day, close your eyes, hold this object in your hand and tune into the feelings in your body. Smile gently and feel warmth and relaxation flood your body as your heart expands outward. Think of a favourite memory and feel your body and heart lighten and soar. Practice this often to naturally experience the divine guidance of Heart Living.

Spend time in your sacred place daily

Spend some gentle, loving time every day in your sacred space. Play some beautiful music or a guided meditation that takes you fully into your heartspace. Then write, draw, create or just sit. Joyfully do whatever your heart calls you to do, and experience Heart Living at its divine, loving finest.

GET YOUR EXTRAORDINARY
FREE GIFT BONUS

Cynthia Zeki is kindly offering a **FREE BONUS GIFT** to all readers of this book.

Heart Living Meditations

Use these meditations to practice Heart Living and use the wisdom and profound love in your heart to unite your left-brain thought with your right-brain creativity. These meditations help you live peacefully and joyfully in Divine Love.

Simply visit the web page below and follow the directions to directly download *Heart Living Meditations*.

www.sparkoftheheart.com

'Trust your life to give you everything
you need to be who you came here to be.
This requires letting go of the attachment to
outcomes and allowing life to unfold ...
Know you are not alone and that there are
no accidents, just lessons.'

Maria Russo

Maria Russo is a licensed clinical social worker with a private psychotherapy practice in the greater Denver area, USA. For the past twenty years she has been helping people in various settings move from a state of surviving into a life of thriving; guiding them to find their own inner goodness and beauty and transform what is no longer working in order to create a more fulfilling and authentic life. She facilitates in her clients the change that is necessary to help them awaken to the many possibilities for personal growth and deep spirituality. Her passion for this work was born of her own experience.

As a child, Maria was surrounded by rich, religious values and traditions which supported what she was born knowing: that we come to this life essentially as spiritual beings to learn how to grow closer to God. By the time she was eight she had a clear vision of how she wanted to dedicate her life by living in a convent.

When she was sent to live with relatives the summer she turned ten, everything changed. Maria fell victim to years of a form of abuse which led her to believe that God saw her now as evil, destroying her dreams.

After many years of wishing her life would magically go back to making sense again, Maria began a new search for meaning. Not knowing where to look, she began by setting intentions, discovering then an emerging pattern. Opportunities started to present themselves for learning, and just the right teachers began to appear. Soon she understood that her eight-year-old child's dream had been an attempt to mould her life into someone else's version of God. She then awakened to the truth that her wounds had led her inward in search of healing, bringing her to her very centre where the Divine resides.

Maria has worked with inmates in correctional facilities, adolescents in residential treatment, families in a private psychiatric hospital, and for the last ten years with victims of alcoholism and drug addiction in outpatient settings. She is working on her first memoir, *The Growing Soul,* to be published in 2012.

The Awakening of a Soul

MARIA RUSSO

Fresh from Heaven

Once I heard about a mother who, after putting her infant down for a nap, noticed her three year old go into the baby's room. Watching unnoticed from the doorway, the mother saw her toddler walk over to the bassinette, stand on her tiptoes and lean toward the baby to whisper, 'Tell me about God. I am starting to forget.'

Many believe that as children we keep the veil that separates us from the other side for several years. It fades slowly as we become conditioned by our families and the beliefs of the world we are born into. Our purpose for choosing a human life slips from our memory, like sand sifting through our fingertips.

As a young child, I had no specific memories of the other side, but I did have a longing for death that was in no way morbid or depressing. It was more like being homesick for something glorious I couldn't really remember, yet was anxious to return to. It came with a knowing that we are essentially spiritual beings and the only reason we come to earth is to learn how to get closer to God.

Everything in my life supported this notion. I was born into a Catholic, Italian family and lived in a neighbourhood where everyone had the same values, customs and outlook on life. Not only did my parents care for me, but I was also loved and nurtured by aunts, uncles, grandparents, nuns, school teachers, priests and the parents of my friends. My role models were the nuns who taught me in the catechism classes I went to twice a week, as well as the nuns at the convent on Best Street where both my mother's sister and her aunt lived behind cloistered walls. I couldn't wait to grow up and dedicate my life to God as they had. When my six-year-old cousin died, I was puzzled by how upset my godparents were. I envied the fact that she was getting to go Home so quickly and wondered how long it would be before God called me back.

Those first ten years of my life were mystical. My dreams were aligned with the longings of my soul. All I ever wanted was an intimate relationship with God. By the time I was eight, I had a well-developed vision of how I would spend my life. I knew I didn't want to go into the cloister order my aunts were in although I loved visiting them every week. Their life of silence and hard work behind a walled-in community did not appeal to me. I was more fascinated by the nuns I heard about who took care of the children at Father Baker's Orphanage. I dreamed of one day becoming the Mother Superior.

I knew without a doubt that God loved me as much as I loved God and that the purpose of life was to live in such a way that earned you the best possible seat in heaven. I was aiming for the right side of the Father.

She talked a lot about sin and how important it was to be good, not happy. 'You can be happy when you go to heaven.'

My spiritual devotion overrode the problems of everyday life. I was only five when my father got sick and was sent to live in a mental hospital. In 1948 that was a life sentence. Once he was stabilised on medication, he was allowed to come home on Wednesday nights for dinner and to spend every weekend with us. So, I didn't feel the full effect of not having my father at home.

Though my mother's heart was broken, she never let my dad's hospitalisation stop her from being a devoted wife, spending as much time as she could at the hospital when he wasn't at home. My mum was a strict disciplinarian and, though unaffectionate, she made sure I always had what I needed. She talked a lot about sin and how important it was to be good, not happy. 'You can be happy when you go to heaven,' she would tell me, 'but you have to be good to get there.' And just to make sure I got the point, she would add, 'Mummy doesn't love bad girls.' I did not feel the full effect of this statement because I knew I was good and that God loved me.

Secrets

The summer I turned ten, everything changed. My mum's own mother had died the Christmas before. So, she decided that the day after school ended we were moving to a rural town thirty miles away where her three sisters lived — leaving my father behind and everyone else I knew and loved.

That summer we moved into an upstairs apartment in a relative's home and my mother made arrangements for me to go to the Catholic school on the other side of town. Then one day, just before school started, she announced, 'You are going to be moving in with your godparents.' The Catholic school was just down the block from them. She didn't tell me the reason I couldn't just live at home and walk the mile or so to school was because she could not afford the tuition for living outside the parish. If she used my godparents' address then I could attend school for free. To say I lived there when I didn't was unthinkable to her.

So, I moved in with an aunt who was immobilised with grief, as her daughter had died four months before, and an uncle who couldn't keep his hands off me. The first time he pulled up my shirt and touched my newly budding breasts was weeks before I actually moved in. I begged my mother to let me stay with her. The subject was not up for negotiation.

I longed for someone to ask me what was wrong, but no one ever did.

My world became filled with trying to protect myself from my uncle who lurked in every corner of the house to catch me alone and came into my bedroom every night. It was 1953 and there was no one to tell. I believed I was the only one in the world this was happening to. Besides, if I did tell, what would that do to my aunt who was already filled with grief? I made a promise to myself that I would never be the source of more pain in her life. I longed for someone to ask me what was wrong, though, forcing me to tell so that whatever happened after that would not be my fault. But no one ever did.

I started to think that everything I once believed just wasn't true and that God hated me. I was confused about whose sin it really was, but I knew that the possibility of going to Heaven was slipping away.

On most days in the fifth grade, I stared out the window, mesmerised by a recurring fantasy about becoming a martyr. The nuns had taught us that if someone gave their life for God, even if they were sinners they would go straight to Heaven. I started to imagine gunmen coming to our school, lining up all the children in the school yard. Then they would point their rifles and demand that everyone deny God or be shot. In my reverie all the children would fall to the ground crying, except me.

The following year, I tried to go to a priest in the confessional just so I could tell somebody, to relieve some of the pressure of my heavy secret. But when I realised he might tell me I had to talk to someone in my family, I took off running because I couldn't take that chance. It would have been unthinkable for me to go against what a priest said.

Then one day it all ended. My mother finally gave in and let me stay at home the year I went into the eighth grade. Somehow I had survived those three years, even though I'd lost more than my innocence. I was sure my once bright soul had become darkened. I felt betrayed and abandoned by God.

A few months later, my deepest fears were validated when my mother told me about 'evil women'. 'When you get married,' she said, 'and your husband puts on his hat to go out the door, you put on your hat and go with him.' Then she added, 'Men cannot help themselves with evil women.' I did not know at the time why it seemed so important for my mum to relay this message about women who can ruin men's lives. Later, though, I learned that one of her brother-in-laws had been having an affair she was trying to justify.

I tried to put two and two together and came up with the belief that God must have created me as one of those evil women. If this is true then I will never be worthy to enter a convent.

By the time I was fifteen, everything I had ever known and loved was gone. I lived alone inside my head, not wanting anyone to find out about 'me'. Yet I did not feel evil. God is wrong about me, I thought, vowing to straighten things out when I grew up.

Growing Up

I made a new plan for my life. I decided that I would show God how wrong He was by marrying a good Catholic man, so He could see my good intentions. I felt confident that this would work because somehow I had gotten the idea that my life would start fresh again when I turned twenty-one and became an adult. So, I hid my feelings behind a smile, no longer wanting anyone to ask me what was wrong.

By the time I was graduating from high school, I longed to go on to college but my mother would not even talk to me about it, telling me that I had to go to work to help her with the bills. She had dropped out of school in the sixth grade and my dad had dropped out in his sophomore year of high school. So, it seemed I had already surpassed any dream either of them had for me.

I hardly ever got to see my dad anymore. He only came home on holidays when someone would drive the thirty miles to pick him up and take him back to the hospital a few days later. My mother took a Greyhound bus faithfully every Sunday to visit him.

When I was nineteen, I decided it was time for me to move out of my mother's home. Before I could make a plan, though, one of my cousins got her own apartment and my mother made it clear that it was a disgrace to the family for a single girl to live on her own. Not being able to handle her judging me like that, I knew I would just have to wait until I got married to move out.

Shortly after my twentieth birthday, I met someone who captured my heart from the first glance. When I learned that he had been in a Catholic school since the first grade and was currently a junior in a Catholic college in a neighbouring state, I felt certain he was the man for me. I knew of his family, having gone to school with his younger sister. His grandmother was prominent in the church community and his mother had converted to Catholicism when she married his father. Even though his father died during World War II, his mother and grandmother made sure he had a strong Catholic upbringing.

When he had to return to school a few weeks after we met, we started a long-distance relationship. After graduation, he took a job hundreds of miles from our hometown, so we never lived in the same city for the three years before we were married. There were many red flags that things were not right between us during that time, but I never doubted my love for him. So, I told myself that as soon as we got married everything would fall into place.

Our wedding was planned for a weekend in May. When he arrived at my front door step a few days before the wedding, I ran to greet him, flinging open the door, expecting to melt into his arms. Instead, I was greeted with anger. 'Why wasn't my grandmother invited to the rehearsal dinner?' he demanded to know.

The tension escalated throughout the weekend. The morning we were to say our vows, I thought about calling off the wedding. But then I thought about how I would be trapped living at home with my mother indefinitely, knowing I did not have the emotional maturity to take a stand in my life. So, I made a conscious decision to go ahead with our plans, convincing myself it was just pre-nuptial jitters and everything would make sense once we were married.

The morning we were to say our vows, I thought about calling off the wedding.

My first disappointment came during the first weekend in our new home. I asked my husband what time we were going to Mass on Sunday. Nothing prepared me for the response I got.

'I lost my religion in college,' he said. 'I don't go to church.' Apparently, he had been putting on an act to please his grandmother. Since the only times we were together were when he was home on vacation, I had only got to see what she saw.

Those first few weeks I went to church alone; but each time it got harder and harder. Nothing was right and I fell into a deep depression. On most days I could barely manage to get myself out of bed. Divorce crossed my mind, but it went against everything I believed in. It would never be an option, I told myself. After a few months, I got a job which distracted me from the disappointment in my life.

When my husband was hired by a large corporation after college, his new employer made it clear that the job was contingent on his agreement to be transferred to different cities around the country wherever he was needed. I also agreed as part of the conditions of our marriage.

The first transfer came about around our first wedding anniversary and the second a year later. By the time we were moving into our third home, I was pregnant with our first child and my depression was as strong as it had been those first six months of marriage. I didn't look for a job because of my pregnancy and now my husband was traveling for business five days a week; I found myself alone most of the time.

In this state, I did not expect to have feelings for my unborn child. But when the doctor told me I had a little girl, I was overwhelmed by feelings of joy that matched what I once felt as a child. Our second daughter was born fifteen months later and life became more stable while we stayed in one place for four years. Two babies one year apart kept me busy. But as much as I loved them, I was unhappy in my marriage and the depression started to creep back in.

With my thirtieth birthday approaching, I began to question why I had not noticed my rite of passage into adulthood. I still felt like a ten year old in many ways. In the books I read as a teenager, there always seemed to be a distinct line that was crossed into adulthood. I never suspected being a 'grown-up' was about anything more than a chronological age. It was the first time I ever considered that maybe I had to do something to help myself.

It was the first time I ever considered that maybe I had to do something to help myself.

Re-Awakening

By the time I turned thirty-one, I was about to give birth to my third daughter and we had just settled after another transfer. Her birth came with deep stirrings within me. I started to see myself through someone else's eyes, as though I was seeing a stranger, and I wondered who I was and what I still believed in.

Then about a year later, on a summer-like day in April, I caught a glimpse of my oldest daughter as if seeing her for the first time. She was six years old and in that moment I saw myself in her. I thought about how excited I had been at her age to be getting old enough to receive my First Holy Communion and how happy my life had been. Then I realised that I was not giving my children the religious foundation I had been given. What will my children do when they grow up and become depressed if they have never known the love of God as I once did? I still carried the hope that one day I would recapture that childhood love. I had not stepped into a church in ten years except for when we went home on vacation or when we had our children baptised.

I still carried the hope that one day I would recapture that childhood love.

The following Sunday, I left the girls with their father and went to the little church at the top of the hill. It was a start. I dared to receive Communion without the benefit of going to Confession, even though I knew it was required of me to first ask for absolution for all my sins. This was something I was going to have to ease into. The one thing I loved the most about church was receiving Communion. I figured the worst that could happen by me going against the church laws was that the Host just wouldn't be sacred for me.

The experience left me with wanting more and I planned to go back the following Sunday. But my husband came home that week with the news that we had been transferred again. I interpreted the timing of this move as a church door slamming in my face and the grandfather/Santa Claus image of God I still had in my head screaming at me, 'You are not welcome here! You are a sinner!' So, even though it would be two months before we had to move, I didn't go back.

We were settled into our new home by summer, and despite the resentment that had been building since my perceived rejection by God, I commenced to look for a Catholic church nearby – for the children. Just because God hated me was no reason to deprive my daughters of a religious education and I just hoped it wasn't too late to get that started. I joined the local church and registered the older two for catechism classes. We started going to Mass that Fall.

As I reluctantly sat in my pew one Sunday, the new priest who had come to the parish that summer walked out onto the pulpit. He drew me in like a magnet, talking about growing out of our sixth grade mentality of religion and developing broader, more adult ways of seeing God. 'You are my new family,' he told us 'and I expect to be invited into your homes and get to know you.' A few weeks later, I called him and asked him to come by and meet us. Then I told my husband, knowing he would be furious. He had a choice whether or not to be home that night, but even though he knew he'd been tricked, he stayed. When the priest showed up in jeans, my husband took to him like an old friend and they filled the evening with talk about fishing! Feeling left out and rejected, I made an appointment with the priest to confess a lifetime of sins in the privacy of his office, which required some soul searching, to make sense of my life.

The night before I was to meet with him, I woke myself up screaming. The dream was hauntingly vivid, as though I were watching a scene from a horror movie. I saw myself as a child, crouched in the far corner of a horse stable trying to make myself invisible. The horse that was looking for me had a straw hat on its head and a cigar in its mouth. There was no doubt about who it was, and I knew I had to wake up before the horse found me or I would be stomped to death.

I had always believed that once I had moved out of my uncle's house and the abuse stopped, that was the end of it. I had no concept of still being affected by what had occurred in any way, but this dream was telling me something different. Confused and drained, I cancelled my appointment with the priest and stayed in bed trying to figure out what was happening to me.

Eventually, I made another appointment and revealed the secrets I had never told anyone before. I wasn't surprised when he told me that I needed more help than what he could give me and handed me the number of a counsellor he recommended; I called the following week to make an appointment.

In just a couple of sessions, I began to unravel the self-loathing that had crept into my life. The counsellor helped me understand the source of my feelings of being stifled and separated from my very soul. He also pointed

'What do you like to do for yourself?' he asked. I couldn't come up with an answer.

out how everything I did revolved around what other people needed from me. 'What do you like to do for yourself?' he asked. I couldn't come up with an answer, but it didn't take me long to catch on. Soon I was inspired to sign up at the local community college for a psychology class I had always wanted to take.

Happy feelings started to re-emerge as I began to pay attention to myself. But then another transfer came all too quick. I was able to finish my semester, but as soon as it ended we were moving again. We have only lived here one year and I am finally getting some help, I thought. The old resentment came back and the message I interpreted this time was God telling me, 'You are not worth saving. You don't deserve to heal.'

We moved the week before Christmas, and once the holidays were behind us I buried myself in the activities of decorating the house and getting the children adjusted to another new home and school. In order to stay close to the priest in our last parish, I had volunteered to work in the food pantry two mornings a week and we had formed a friendly relationship. He stayed in touch with me after we left through occasional letters. Then one day I received a short note in the mail. 'I have some time off in May,' he wrote, 'and would like to come to visit for a couple of days.' I responded quickly and made the necessary plans. He had helped me in so many ways and now I was going to get a chance to let him see how far I had come.

During the two and one half days he was with us, I was able to see myself through his eyes and it made me realise that I still had much to work on and heal. When I took him back to the airport early Saturday morning, I knew I had failed somehow. I didn't feel we had connected like I had hoped. The tears started before I made it home and they virtually did not stop until a month later.

Going Deeper

I was thirty-five years old and had what looked like a picture-perfect life – the four-bedroom colonial in the suburbs, the latest model car in the driveway, summer vacations and winter getaways. My executive husband worked to support us and I took care of everything else. I blended into the fabric of everyone else's lives, doing what was expected of me with no sense of who I was or what I wanted.

Then one sunny morning in June, my three year old crawled up into my lap, wrapping her little arms around me. 'Don't cry, mommy,' she said. 'Don't cry.' I loved my children, but for the past four weeks not only could I not stop crying, I also could not stop thinking of ending my life. I never made a plan. I knew even if I did I would never go through with it, but I couldn't get past the feeling of wanting to die.

After lunch that day, I put my daughter down for her afternoon nap and went to my room to cry alone. But her innocent, three-year-old wisdom had profoundly touched me. A voice came from deep within me. 'You know you are just getting sicker and sicker, Maria,' it said. I knew that was true, and in a moment I also knew I didn't want to die; I just wanted to be rescued.

No one has ever asked me what is wrong, I thought.

'Start where you are. Help yourself,' the voice continued.

'I can go to a psychiatrist,' I said out loud.

I blended into the fabric of everyone else's lives, doing what was expected of me with no sense of who I was or what I wanted.

The habitual need to fall deeper into a depression, in the hope that someone would notice and do whatever they could to pull me out, started to dissipate. I thought about how my father got stuck in a mental hospital for eighteen years and I knew that is not what I wanted. I just wanted someone to recognise my sadness, to validate my feelings and make me feel better. I became aware that while having this conversation with myself, the tears had stopped.

When I told my husband about my decision to see a doctor, he refused to support it, perhaps fearing I might expose something wrong with him along with my own sins. Although disappointed, I had already begun feeling relief since making my decision and knew I would find another way.

As it turned out, it found me.

A New Beginning

A week or two later, a flyer came in the mail from the local community college. I had thought about taking a college class again in the fall as one way to do something for myself. I scoured the schedule for classes that would begin in September. And there it was: Personal Growth 101, including private counselling.

The summer seemed particularly long that year, but finally the first day of class arrived. It was held in a stand-alone building on campus that didn't look like a traditional classroom. The desks were set up so that the class sat in a circle. The instructor was a man in his early fifties, with greying red hair and piercing blue eyes. He handed each of us a 12-page syllabus and started explaining what we could expect over the next three months.

I was uncomfortable during the first class as I looked around at the other students who seemed immature, introverted and unable to speak above a whisper. They were half my age, with the exception of one other woman who dropped out the second week.

I tried to ignore everyone else in the room except for our instructor, a student development specialist. I learned later that the class was mandatory for the students who did not test well on a readiness test to get into a community college.

'This course was designed as an experimental group in which you will be using resources, personal journals, testing, and small group activities and discussions to actively be involved in the process of your own growth,' he stated. 'The basic assumption is not that you have a problem, but that you have come to learn something about yourself.' He continued, 'Though this task is perhaps the most agonising, it will be the most beautiful task of your life because through it you will get in touch with yourself at a much richer level than you might have otherwise. The idea is that the more you are yourself, the more you are able to enrich your life.'

He asked us to follow through the syllabus with him as he pointed out the four major units of the class. 'There are three objectives in the first unit of developing a positive concept of self,' he said, going on to identify them as firstly exploring and clarifying personal values, then determining the primary motivations underlying our behaviour, and finally personal goal-setting and decision-making. As I listened to him talk, this feeling of gratitude washed over me for having the desire to look in a community college flyer in the first place and then to find exactly what I needed at exactly the right time. I couldn't believe how much better this was going to be than an hour a month in a psychiatrist's office. He became not only my teacher but my therapist as well. I met with him weekly in his office for individual attention.

He taught me how to use Ira Progoff's Intensive Journal as a therapeutic tool, told me that I had goodness and beauty inside me and pointed out that I was 'tragically unprepared' for life. Because I had believed that there was something terribly wrong with me that could maybe never be fixed, I welcomed the concept of 'unprepared', which encouraged me to believe I could do something about it.

He told me that I had goodness and beauty inside me and pointed out that I was 'tragically unprepared' for life.

My new confidante had been in the seminary, leaving just before ordination to become a priest because there were certain things about the Catholic religion he just could not accept. Not only did he have an amazing ability to understand archetypes and human behaviour, but he also understood my spiritual angst.

My husband did not get transferred for three years. I continued in therapy beyond the class, learning to uncover the irrational beliefs that were directing my life, becoming more honest about what I wanted and was capable of achieving. I learned, as well, all the ways in which my relationship with my mother had affected me and discovered how much my father meant to me despite his illness. I achieved a high level of insight and gained many tools to go inward and explore my very soul.

By the time we were transferred again, resentment was reshaping into gratitude as I started to recognise a pattern forming where we would move when I was ready for the next teacher that Life was to present to me. The second year into this move, I awoke with great excitement on New Year's Day, 1983, realising it was the year I would turn forty. I thought about how, for the first twenty years of my life, I had tried to be as good as I could to please my mother. Then for the next twenty years, I fell into the same role with my husband who was just as demanding and immovable as my mother. 'If I am lucky enough to live until I am sixty,' I told myself, 'that means I have another twenty years from now, and I am claiming them for me!' I decided that morning that I was going to give myself the best possible birthday present that summer by becoming all that I could be.

Some of the things I wanted to pursue were going to be uncomfortable for my husband. He was already feeling the effects of my growth and it caused a lot of tension in our home. But determined to continue, the first thing I did was commit to a Renewal Weekend Workshop later that month at the church I was now attending regularly. The experience gave me permission to drop the things in my religion that no longer served me and showed me a softer side of God. I found another community college to take classes and another counsellor to help me address some of the issues both from my childhood and within my marriage.

By the time my birthday neared, I decided that my present to myself was going to be a college education. I set my sights on an Associate Degree in Human Services. But during the first semester in a Human Development class, I discovered that I wanted a graduate degree. By the spring of 1985, I was a full-time student with a psychology major in a four year university program. A whole new world had opened up to me.

In my first full year, I took two semesters of Honours History and two semesters of Honours Philosophy. There were no text books and no tests in these classes. Instead, we read literature and wrote papers in response to what we had read and engaged in deep, philosophical discussions.

As a result, I grasped the difference between religion and spirituality, and everything started to make sense.

I learned more about religion in the first semester of History than I ever imagined was possible to learn. The foundation of my belief system cracked open when I learned that Catholicism did not even begin until about three hundred years after Jesus walked the earth, and only then because the Roman Empire needed something to bring the people together, not having any other popular religion at the time. In my second semester philosophy class, Existentialism, we focused mostly on Nietzsche, reading and discussing *Thus Spake Zarathustra.* As a result, I grasped the difference between religion and spirituality, and everything started to make sense. When Nietzsche said 'God is Dead', he meant the personified God that man created in his own image. I began to understand God as a Divine Presence rather than a person.

My whole life came alive with possibilities.

Fascinated by the Renaissance, I learned that many people were in search of the Truth of how life should be lived and many found what they were looking for, though in different ways.

Plato's Allegory of the Cave helped me to understand how my mother saw things a certain way, trying to pass down the shadows on the cave wall to me as absolute Truth, not knowing she was chained to someone else's false beliefs.

My whole life came alive with possibilities. I also became aware of my marriage as something that interfered with my growth; I was feeling spiritually strangled by my husband. The more I learned and the more I spoke up for myself, the more he tried to control me. I wanted him to be happy with me, but instead he felt threatened and scared that too much was changing.

As we approached our twentieth wedding anniversary, I made a decision. Either we were going to renew our vows and begin a new phase in our relationship where there was mutual respect for each other's goals or we were going to divorce. I was no longer willing to fight for who I was or to stifle the parts of me that he could not handle.

We both worked as best we could in trying to incorporate new ways of being together, with neither of us wanting to end the marriage. But despite our valiant efforts, our marriage was not meant to survive. We filed for divorce.

A Deeper Understanding

Just as life has a purpose, so do relationships. I believe that my husband was the perfect mate for me all those years precisely because he was emotionally unavailable. All my life I had been searching for answers outside of myself. He was an important instrument in my search for God because of how our life together forced me to go inward to find my answers. By honouring my own life, I honoured his.

About five years later, he married a woman more suitable for him. When our oldest daughter got married sixteen years after we divorced, he pulled me aside at the wedding reception to thank me for being strong enough to follow my heart all those years before. 'I only hope you are as happy in your life today as I am in mine,' he said, giving me a hug.

The path to living life to its fullest is going to look different for everyone. My path took me down a road that ended in divorce because that was necessary for both my husband and me to discover a way to free ourselves from the distortions we were left with from our early years. Motivated by what I knew was possible, I led the way. Neither of us knew at the time that divorce was going to be just the thing that my husband needed to discover the difference between 'settling for' and 'finding' what happiness meant for him.

Once I let go of the way I thought things should be unfolding and embraced what was, I was able to leave the past behind and live in harmony with my own divine purpose, entering into the dance with Life and marrying my longing.

Today I have an amazing life. I have learned to trust the Universe to know my intentions and respond to my needs. I no longer jump to conclusions when things seem to be going differently than I expected, but trust that all things lead to my highest good. I feel at one with my life's purpose and find great joy through helping others do the same.

I find myself in a wonderfully spiritual part of the country, in the midst of a metaphysical community with a spiritual message that is an answer to my childhood yearning for deep,

Maria happy in her amazing life in Denver

meaningful connection with the Divine. I had no way of knowing when I first moved to this mile-high city that it would be the fulfilment of a dream in so many ways. But my life led me to this wonderful place that serves my spirit with its many great teachers.

I have come to believe that every challenge I have ever been given to face has been carefully selected just for me in order to learn what I came here to learn. For example, I believe that one of my deeper lessons in this lifetime is to truly internalise the meaning of forgiveness. What else would have motivated me to work so hard at this lesson if I had not been given something horrendous to forgive? That is how our wounds become our greatest blessings.

Trust your life to give you everything you need to be who you came here to be. This requires letting go of the attachment to outcomes and allowing life to unfold. Let God surprise you! Know you are not alone and that there are no accidents, just lessons. Recognise the patterns in your life that lead you to your own joy. Sometimes it takes a lot of unlearning to see the good that is flowing through our experience.

Know you are first and foremost a spiritual being. Rely on your intuition, the whisperings of your heart. Listen to the still, small voice within that guides you. If I had not listened to my own inner voice when I decided to help myself right where I was – instead of getting sicker and waiting for someone to throw me a lifeline – I would not have been led to the life-changing experience I had in my Personal Growth class.

Most of all, I encourage you to honour your life by spending time each day in solitude and quiet. Find a spiritual practice that feels right for you, whether it be journaling, meditation, long walks in nature, spending time with animals or the like. Cultivate your own relationship with the loving presence that neither judges nor condemns. Be present in every moment, learning from the past and allowing the future to unfold as it will in time.

Suggestions to Help You Live Extraordinarily by Uncovering the Longings of Your Soul

Explore your true feelings and honour them

Close your eyes and remember what it was like when you were a child. What were the things that you liked to do that were not the ideas of well-meaning parents, friends or teachers – the things that you thought of all on your own? What did you get into trouble for? What kinds of risks were you willing to take to do what you wanted to do? We all have something that we are passionate about that brings us joy, but sometimes we lose sight of it. Make a date with yourself several times a week to explore your true feelings in a way that is meaningful to you. It could be fifteen minutes a day if that is all you can fit in your busy schedule. Just begin. Honour yourself by taking a walk in nature, journaling, meditating, reading inspirational books or listening to music that speaks to you. The idea is to practice cultivating a relationship with your inner being.

Look for the blessings

As you go deeper into your life, start to identify the blessings that have come from your most challenging experiences. This may not be clear at first. It will take practice. Start by writing down your missteps, your accomplishments, your turning points. What were the crossroads you have faced and which direction did you choose? Freely write in your journal about the path you didn't take. Examine your expectations. Are you holding onto judgments or grudges? Do you need to learn to forgive yourself and others to set your soul free? Sometimes the things you had to learn to do as a child in order to survive are no longer serving you, but they are all you know. Be mindful. The idea is to live in the present, allowing the past to be what it is: the magnificent foundation for who you are becoming. The exercises in my free eWorkbook are designed to help you identify what might be keeping you stuck, preventing you from moving into your full power and most extraordinary life.

 ## *Join a network or similar interest group*

As you begin to discover the desires of your heart that have most likely been lying dormant for some time, seek the company of those who inspire you and share your interests. If writing is your forte, join a creative writing group. If it is acting, find a class or help out at a local theatre. If serving in your community is something that calls to you, check out volunteer opportunities. The idea is to find a network to support you as you learn more about yourself and what you really want.

GET YOUR EXTRAORDINARY
FREE GIFT BONUS

Maria Russo is kindly offering a **FREE BONUS GIFT** to all readers of this book.

The Journey Inward

An eWorkbook containing exercises to guide you in expanding the awareness of your innate goodness and beauty, cultivating a deeper relationship with your Innermost Self, discovering your wounds as sacred portals to a more meaningful life and nourishing your soul with unconditional self-love.

Simply visit the web page below and follow the directions to directly download *The Journey Inward*.

www.mariarussolcsw.com

'I understood way back then that
fear is an inevitable companion.
It was with me regardless.
What mattered most was
my relationship with it.'

Cath Edwards

Cath Edwards is the Director of Yes You Can Coaching International Pty Ltd. Well into her fabulous fifties, which she calls 'Mid Life Happiness' instead of the 'Mid Life Crisis', she has worked in many different settings – including government and non-government managerial positions – watching and understanding what makes people tick. She is also a mother and grandmother with a track record in drawing on her own courage and confidence during some very challenging journeys, including the big 'C' where she was faced with the possibility of life without a nose! Through it all, Cath has succeeded to live an extraordinary life that is an amazing tapestry of colour and dimension.

Cath has a passion for assisting people of all ages and experiences to transform their lives as well – to create their own beautiful tapestry. She firmly believes that no matter what change you want to see in your life, the place you must begin to work is within. As a certified Performance Coach, Life Coach, NLP Practitioner, Matrix Therapist and Hypnotherapist, Cath works alongside and mentors her clients as they turbocharge past fears and challenges that they never believed possible.

Cath's clients have experienced amazing results where they have quit smoking, lost weight, improved their image and self-confidence, started a new and amazing career or business, built remarkable relationships, dropped points off their golf score, quit biting their nails and grinding their teeth, and stressed way less! Cath runs a range of workshops and webinars that embrace the stages in women's lives that offer significant and life-changing challenges and where fear can abound in bucket loads. The workshops move participants through transformational change with a variety of activities, 'good ol' natters', stress busters and networking opportunities.

The motto of Cath Edwards and Yes You Can Coaching International is 'The winner in life thinks in terms of *I can, I will, I am.*'

The Secret to an Extraordinary Life is to Fall Down Seven Times and Get up Eight

CATH EDWARDS

I can clearly recall the day my surgeon told me that there was a strong chance that my entire nose would be removed as a result of invasive skin cancer. Surgery was scheduled. It was certainly one of the most defining moments of my life. All the scary details were explained to me about how I had no choice and if they didn't act swiftly the cancer would invade the rest of my face. I was sitting there in his surgery with all the 'what ifs' ahead of me. As I left his office, I was reminded of my fate by a few elderly and very facially-deformed women sitting in the waiting room. I walked slowly to my car, sat down and gave myself permission to cry. I was a few months away from turning the 'Magic 40'. I wasn't old, not even close. I had my life to live.

What if I didn't have a nose for my fortieth birthday celebrations? What if I couldn't work again? What if my husband wasn't attracted to me anymore? What if no one could ever look at me again without being repulsed? What if all my dreams would be shattered? What about my kids; how would this affect them? How would I have a conversation with anyone without being self-conscious? Hang on, let's backtrack a bit. Did he really mean my whole nose? As in 'no nose to speak of', gone and never to come back again?

You see, my whole face was a 'hotchpotch' of three different types of skin cancer. There was one area, not in my nose, that had the potential to spread to other parts of my body and potentially threaten my life. It was removed many years ago and to this day I still fear it will return to my neck or my brain. On another part of my face there is a rare form of skin cancer that keeps growing back because it has little satellites that can spring up on any part of the face or neck. Sometimes I would go to bed at night and have dreams that they removed my entire face and replaced it with another one from someone who had died. You know, like those amazing stories they have on the news about people who have their faces totally replaced.

The doctors were hedging on a total nose removal to offset the spread of cancer into my brain or my facial bones. Strangely enough, I wasn't too concerned about the cancer that was life-threatening on the other part of my face or those weird little cancer satellites; to me they were small and distant in comparison to the removal of my nose.

What I was really distressed about was the damage that the removal of the cancer on my nose was going to do to my appearance, my ability to work and my relationships with others. By this stage, I had already undergone a number of operations to remove cancer on my face. There were no other options. It was have the cancer removed or watch it slowly penetrate all aspects of my face. It was capable of invading my eyes, my ears, my jaw and my mouth. But I was tossing up what would be worse, life-threatening skin cancer or losing my nose!

To put it bluntly, I was sh*t scared. I didn't know anyone who had been through this experience, and when I asked one of my doctors if counselling was available for my emotional issues about deformity, regrettably I was thrown the off-hand response, 'I don't know what you are worried about; you should be thankful that we are getting rid of the cancer, and no, we don't have anything like that available.'

Wham!

I remember that when the doctor was saying this, I was privately thinking: *You are not me. You don't know how I feel and you are clearly not interested in what I feel. I'm just another patient, a medical number. You don't want to feel my pain. You are safe if I don't speak up and show my feelings. My fear is not yours and you will not let it be yours.* In fact, I was enraged.

I knew the shock of looking in the mirror after the bandages are removed.

I had already had plenty of previous experience with facial surgery, with five lengthy operations to remove skin cancer. I knew the shock of looking in the mirror after the bandages are removed. I can vividly remember the surgeon locking the door to my hospital room, giving me the mirror and asking me to take my time and tell him what I thought. Oh man! How do you tell your surgeon that it looks like an incredible mess, with all those lines and stitches going everywhere and my nose pulling to the left, completely out of shape?

I also knew all about the stitches opening up and haemorrhaging. I knew about sleeping upright to reduce the pain and swelling, and all about the vomiting after the anaesthetic. And I was well aware of the time it takes to heal on the outside.

But about this next big challenge, I knew nothing. I wasn't sure how long I would take to heal on the outside, but more importantly, on the inside. You see, I don't think I understood everything going on at the time, but one thing was certain: I was definitely feeling it all. And what did I do with those feelings? Well, at this point, I was beginning to build my emotional jail, though I didn't realise it. Whatever pain I endured, I would take it inside and lock it in. My fear was mine, and it was crippling for some time.

Closing the Door on Emotions

This jail proved to be an effective 'hidey hole' for my emotions on many an occasion after this. I underwent a total of twenty-five hours of surgery over a number of years following that initial diagnosis. I remember before I went in for one of the first operations, where I was to have a large flap of skin pulled from one side of my face over a large hole in my nose, they drew all over my face to show the part that would be removed and which parts would be filling the hole. (Yes! I didn't have to lose the nose then after all – though it's still on the cards. More about that later.)

Following this operation, I was healing nicely and thought I needed some help from the beauty counter at a department store. It's like a candy shop of beauty – they can decrease wrinkles, turn back the clock, highlight the colour in your eyes, camouflage uneven skin tone and give a 'pick me up'. I thought they might be able to help me with my scars from that first operation. I think there were about one hundred sutures in total, inside and outside my nose. And I must say that the surgeon did a brilliant job.

I excitedly drove off to the store to find a sympathetic ear and to get some makeup that would (hopefully) do an amazing job of covering up my suture lines. I was feeling optimistic and energised. I wanted to return to work and get on with my life. The beauty consultant was a really nice person, and, I might add, quite beautiful. As she looked at me while I was talking, her colour promptly faded and she passed out. Not the fall-down-and-collapse type of passing out, but her legs went wobbly and she slid down to the floor. She was helped up and out the back to get some water and comfort. Meanwhile, another beautician came out and profusely apologised for the 'fainter'.

I knew it was my face that had made her pass out. She had been looking at the sutures while we chatted about my experience, and that's when it happened. I think the idea of cancer and sutures were a bit much for her. I was shattered, but I didn't show it and I just kept on. I chatted with the other beautician, bought some product and made a mad dash for the car where no one would look at me – all without showing any emotion. My emotional jail was intact. No key to be found by anyone. I had the secret to opening the door and was well versed in getting out of jail later.

I knew it was my face that had made her pass out.

Now, back to the nose.

'OK, Cath,' I had said to myself after the doctor's prognosis. 'Slow it down. Take a back seat. Gather your emotions. The doctor said there was a strong chance that your nose would be removed. It wasn't definite.' But in the hopeful 'off-chance' that it would happen, I did some research; I was looking for more certainty.

The research I conducted about skin cancer and surgery was extensive and hard-nosed (sorry for the pun). I could have received an MBA in 'All things untrue and suss' delivered by the internet. What happens when you lose your nose? Have you ever met anyone without a nose? Is there a No Nose Club? This was all a bit new to me. After finding a reputable medical site, I discovered with shock and horror that they remove your nose to not just prevent the cancer from spreading to elsewhere on your face, but also into your brain.

I had a 'knowing' about the cancer and when I told the surgeon that the cancer was back, there was no physical evidence.

I first discovered I had invasive cancer on my nose when they performed a biopsy on a tiny little red spot on the end of my nose. The spot was so small the surgeon had trouble seeing it and all the subsequent cancers that came along. In fact, I had a 'knowing' about the cancer and when I told the surgeon that the cancer was back, there was no physical evidence. He believed me, asked me to point to the spot, and put a texta colour mark on it. He performed a biopsy and, sure enough, it was invasive skin cancer – again.

I then discovered that when your nose is removed, it takes at least eighteen months to get another one. WOW. Another one! Where does that nose come from? Does someone give it to me? I don't know what your thoughts are at the moment but mine were wild, scared and definitely in great search of certainty.

What did all this mean to me as a woman? Millions of dollars are spent on the beauty industry every year by women in search of beauty. Women crave beauty and youth. Where did I fit in? Was this going to determine who I was and what I would become? Would I be ugly, without beauty? Without beauty, without belonging, without the love of my husband? Who would I become? My need for certainty was large and ever-present at this time, while all I had ever wanted was variety and to live life to the full.

It may have crossed your mind by now to ask whether or not I was a habitual sun worshipper. This definitely wasn't the case. Yes, just like everyone else at that time, I was exposed to the sun – and maybe just like you now! At this point, I would like to suggest, no insist, that if you haven't had your skin checked recently that you put this book down right now and make an appointment. If it is late at night, write it down on your To-Do List and make the appointment first thing in the morning. Use your fear constructively and efficiently. If you are using tanning beds, please stop now. If there is a suspicious lump or mark on your skin, hold the fear, thank it politely as it tries to run wild with the 'What ifs' and give yourself the biggest opportunity to be around – if it is a positive result – and have it checked. No one can do this for you. Only you can master this decision like the many others you will face in your lifetime. Also, don't forget to limit your time in the sun and use protection with sunscreen, hats and shade. Believe it or not, it will also keep you looking younger. I am all for that.

Anyway, here are the gory details I discovered in my research about what would be entailed in my possible nose job, um, nose removal. Well, not all the details because you may be reading this with a 'cuppa' and I do want you to keep reading – I have so much to share.

I learned that I would need a graft from my scalp to my nose cavity and in the interim I would wear glasses with a prosthetic nose. It conjured up images of Groucho Marx for me. Not sure why. Didn't he have a one-liner like this? … 'I never forget a face, but in your case, I'll be glad to make an exception.'

Anyway, the graft grows hair; there is no nose to start with but a graft with hair growing on it in the middle of the face. This was certainly not an appealing prospect to me. I looked at some results for people who had gone through this and … it didn't look good … It didn't even look reasonable. Who were these people? Circus Show freaks. Monsters! So, my little peek into the future wasn't a promising one. I was back in the jail, full of fear. I knew I had the key to open the door. I knew my courage, confidence and perseverance was the key; it was just a matter of opening the door.

My little peek into the future wasn't a promising one. I was back in the jail, full of fear.

What scared me more than anything was the idea that for a whole eighteen months I wouldn't be able to be in the public eye. (I was secretly thinking I wouldn't be able to be in anyone's eye.) Being in the public eye was a major part of my job at the time; I was in the local paper regularly, spoke at national conferences and conducted many, many meetings and community events. I loved being with people – and still do. It's what makes me tick.

Either way, when you are a woman or in the public eye frequently, the thought of scarring and deformity on your face is truly overwhelming.

You see, I had already spent my whole life overwhelmed by scars. I was one of those unlucky adolescents that started the change into adulthood with cystic acne. The cysts seemed to appear overnight, right at a time in my life when I was ready to explore the world and my potential. One minute I had clear skin, the next minute ... brutality and the cruelness of cystic acne. In my mind these cysts were like tennis balls. I spent my adolescence with medical specialists who at that time wouldn't put me on the pill to control the hormonal imbalance. If they were Catholics, it was against their religion to put a young 14-year-old girl on the pill – though it was fine for me to be scarred for life. And the rest of the doctors didn't really have suitable treatment to effectively control the cysts. What they did deprive me of was chocolate and other lovely food, and this gave me lots of guilt about what I ate. They experimented with damaging chemicals and they even suggested that bananas may be causing the problem. I just love bananas.

In many ways the acne scars defined who I was: the girl with the bad acne. But the real scars were hidden deep within. Can you imagine the ridicule at school, boys calling me crusty or lumpy or something else that would make me shudder. To cope, I decided to think that at least I have a chance at doing well at school academically, so maybe that will be who I become – someone who does well at school. Not real cool but it would do. This was contrived by me as settling for something – though I didn't really want this as my label. I also didn't want to be known as the girl with the bad acne. Who did I want to become? I wanted to be remembered as the girl who loved life and had a bagful of things to achieve. I wanted to be carefree and outgoing and living life to its fullest – to feel it and own it. In some ways, my predicament created a steely determination in me way back then. I had a choice – and I made it: I excelled at my school work and I loved life.

It was, undoubtedly, very challenging to move ahead with those ideas when I had difficulty even having eye contact with people. Communication is everything, isn't it? People's eyes are the window to their soul. But I moved way beyond that fear. I suppose I pretended to everyone around me that I was okay and not affected. Of course, I was affected, but not all of it in a bad way. It helped me to create the person I am, and I am proud to say I have achieved many of the dreams of my youth. I knew there was so much more for me. I looked for and found it, and more often than not I fumbled and then started again … and again. It is a life's work. Anton Chekhov says 'A man is what he believes' and I believed I could be somebody; I would grow and contribute to the world in some small way.

Manage the Fear: Your State of Mind

I understood way back then that fear is an inevitable companion. It was with me regardless. What mattered most was my relationship with it. Just think about this for a moment. As an adolescent I could have locked myself up in my bedroom and lost the tremendous opportunities ahead of me. What I now know is that all those years ago I chose to manage my state of mind because what I wanted up ahead of me was so much greater than the pain I was experiencing at the time. I didn't want to miss out. My fear of missing out was greater than my fear of not. By God, I wasn't going to!

The truth be known, there was of course a part of me that was crippled emotionally in my youth and during my facial surgeries, a private part of me. And I still see the scars, both the acne scars and the scars from the nose surgery, every day when I look in a mirror, and even without one. And that is okay. Really it is. The moments are fleeting and are not the pivotal force within me; the scars are merely external. It's amazing how I can look in a mirror and, with a really good angle, not see them at all. I have discovered that the mind is truly amazing, and tricking my own mind is 'cool'. I think and then I create the language I want around those thoughts. First, I speak to myself and then I 'speak' out loud with my actions. I believe and therefore it is real. It's a powerful experience.

The scars are still there but they are managed within my state of mind. If they ever became the sum total of who I am, I would feel helpless, hopeless and powerless, with no possibilities, no change and no choice. This would rob me of all my energy. Instead, I chose, and still choose, to see myself full of energy, with bright colours moving and buzzing and shaping my future.

Let's be clear here. The physical scars are real for me and indisputable. But it's what I do with them that count. I have started to see them in the light of opposites; having long hair or short hair, curly or straight, clear skin or damaged skin. Life is a list of contradictions and opposites, agreements and similarities. It's fine for the scars to be real and for me to want more in my life, rather than the scars being the sum of me. Head down, turned down mouth, nothing to dream of and nothing to look forward to. No thanks. My choice is to have more and be more, to develop to my full potential regardless and to show people, including you, how to do that.

This management or 'book-keeping' of my state of mind has continued for most of my life. Sometimes I get surprised by a challenge I face that initially seems large and ominous; sometimes I am tense and lose my way. Like all of us, I am a work in progress. The strange thing I remember is that in all those doctors' visits and treatments, not one doctor, not one, actually asked me how I was feeling about myself and never once did they mention the long term scars. It wasn't their face, or their fear I suppose, and so to them it didn't matter. Next patient please! So I learnt how to deal with it all myself, including how to use the fear.

In all those doctors' visits and treatments, not one doctor, not one, actually asked me how I was feeling about myself.

The thing is I let the fear be my companion in a way that allowed me to move forward on my terms. If I had waited for the emotion to pass and the fear to subside, I wouldn't be sitting here now, able to share my most extraordinary life with you.

Circumstances, Choices and Control

You see, there has been a litany of fear and trauma throughout my life beyond the adolescent skin problems and cancer surgery on my face. I'll summarise quickly before I get to the extraordinary way I have dealt with life: I lost my first baby at sixteen weeks; I nearly lost my first child at eight weeks after bed rest for the entire pregnancy; I have had surgery on other parts of my body – a long list that will bore you now; I have been injured and subsequently in pain; I have lost my job from an injury; I have fought for my rights in court; and I nearly died in a dental chair. Oh, and I nearly died having heart surgery … And, of course, there was the threat of losing my nose in the midst of all of this.

Now, I could have allowed any of these defining moments to take me down and keep me down. However, that was not a place where I was prepared to stay. I made that choice.

I ask you now, what choices are you making about your life? Are you in an emotional jail surrounded by 'shoulds', 'coulds' and 'have nots'? Are they locked neatly inside? Are you feeling a sense of failure, disappointment and needless frustration? Do you know there is more and that you could give more of yourself? Try these words out for a change.

I can

I will

I am

I can see you lifting your shoulders, feeling courageous and confident. When you speak the language of possibility, it is powerful – YOU are powerful.

When you speak the language of possibility, it is powerful – YOU are powerful.

I learnt to control the things that I could control – the things within me. I forgot about the things outside my control when I was busy making a life. My energies went within, which created more energy outside of myself. I cultivated promises and dreams and threw all my energy within (inside my jail). I then found the key that promised to open the jail door. It was always within me. It was … courage, confidence and perseverance in the face of fear … The fear was just the fuel.

My key: courage + confidence + perseverance

Have you locked yourself in an emotional jail? Are you looking for the key? Believe it or not, it is inside you right now. Dig deep and you will find it. It might be a different shape to mine. It might be fancy with gold and ribbons or it might be like mine, straight up on one side, some scratches and dents with a few smooth curved bits.

The fear will always be ever present. Will people approve? Will they still love me if I do things differently? Will I fail? Am I good enough? Do I belong? Am I truly loved? Are you prepared to see the naked truth? Are you prepared to see your unique qualities, your possibilities and your resources? The fear I have experienced over the course of my life so far is what has given me challenges out of the ordinary, the mundane and the boring – challenges that I was blessed to face. Every step brought me closer to seeing myself for who I am. I was different yet the same as others. I had the deep desire to be loved, to be good enough and to belong in the best way I knew how. I was a speck in the universe but with the inner power to go beyond it, to become more than just a speck.

There are so many women I have met in my life who are holding themselves back. They are in their own emotional jail, scared to speak out because they might see the possibilities. If they do see them, they may have to act. If they act, they may have to be in the dream rather than looking on. Most women I know don't understand fear and their relationship to it. I try to make them realise that it's scary, sure, but then again it's not. It provides opportunities, new ideas and challenges to the boring, boring everyday existence that many women face. By finding your inner courage and confidence, and persevering, you can unlock your emotional jail and walk through the door.

I wanted more than an existence; I wanted 'It' – something special in life.

I wanted more than an existence; I wanted 'It' – something special in life. And I was, and am, prepared to give it a go. Okay, I don't bungy jump and probably never will. I'm not jumping out of planes and swimming through dark underwater caves. They are not a part of my dreams, or what some people refer to as their 'bucket list'. I am not talking about an adrenalin rush. If that 'floats your boat', that's fine. What I am really talking about here is the adrenalin that comes with fear that moves you forward instead of keeping you still, treading water as you hang on until someone tells you to keep swimming or swim backwards. I have only an intellectual understanding of the concept of going backwards, as I know that it's something I choose not to do. The small glimpses I have had have shown me that it's not a good feeling. It removes all possibilities. I also know that I don't want to stay in one spot. If I'm not growing, I am dying. I choose not to die in an emotional jail.

I ask you to think about your emotional jail. How much more pain out of the ordinary can you bear? If your fears are keeping you safe, they are most likely also keeping you from taking risks, making mistakes, stepping up and living an extraordinary life. Imagine having a fear of the extraordinary yet grabbing it with both hands and going for the ride. What is it that you really want from your life? Is fear holding you back?

I believe that over my life I have demonstrated courage and confidence to have the life I desire. Having this courage and confidence is not the absence of fear but my willingness to take action despite its existence. I have learned that you cannot have courage, confidence and perseverance unless you take action. And when you do, it is an empowering feeling. Even when I write this, I feel taller than I really am. I feel strong and real.

Cath playing and enjoying life.

Finding the Key

So, I found the key for my emotional challenges; I found the internal resources, my special key, that I needed to open the door – and I stepped out; I created an attitude and then created the steps. Sure, I tripped a few times. Sometimes I spun in circles, and at other times I quietly retreated to reconnect with my purpose. But I was still taking action to get out of the jail, and with courage and confidence by my side I made a feast of it. If I had waited for the courage, confidence and perseverance to arrive, or someone to give it to me on a platter, I would still be that fragile, emotional teenager and that young woman just about to turn the Magic 40 with nowhere to go but safely tucked up in her jail. I would be certain about my future, certain that everything would stay the same, maybe even slip backwards, with little growth and very little contribution toward my needs as a human being.

Safe? Yes, but still scared. Happy and content? Definitely not. Worried

111

still? You bet. If I had waited for courage, confidence and
ppear before my eyes, I would have been doomed and
felt the amazing experience of the jail opening with the
key that was especially designed for me. I can share my key with you, but it
will always be mine to keep as it only fits into the door of
my emotional jail.

Your own magical mixture of courage, confidence and
perseverance is sitting quietly within you – your magic
key. It is ever present, steadfast and calm. It is wondering
why you have taken so long to acknowledge its existence
and encourage it to come forth so you can utilise its power.

*Imagine
fear and
courage
being
reconciled.*

It is in fact your lifeline from the dull and boring you may be experiencing.
Your multi-faceted key just needs to be introduced to fear. Imagine fear and
courage being reconciled. You give permission for courage to take a leap of
faith. It runs straight past fear, turns around and gives an understanding
smile about what lies ahead. Growth is waiting … and all the possibilities for
a life worth living. And there are no regrets … even about the mistakes that
inevitably happen along the way. My mistakes were my champions.

When I heard the news about my nose, I could have given in. I could
have put avoiding fear ahead of my true desires. I wanted to be a great
role model for my children; I wanted to keep my marriage alive. I could
have prevented myself from truly appreciating and loving my life while
sentenced to my emotional prison. My choice was clear.

What has made my life extraordinary is the way I have dealt with and
utilised my fears in an out-of-the-ordinary way, which led me to live
extraordinarily, going beyond my circumstances.

What are You Focussing on?

My focus was all about what I **wanted** in life; not what I didn't want. I
know that when I concentrated on the idea of losing beauty, that's what
came my way … and some very scary thoughts. What a surprise. What you
focus on is what you get. The more I would concentrate on it, the more
clues and ideas presented themselves that held me back. If I had allowed,
I would have only found the opposite of beauty and the opposite of being

loved or good enough and not belonging. So, I shifted the focus. I changed gears, experimented, took risks, and it was fun. It gave me possibilities again instead of landing back in jail without a Get-Out-of-Jail-for-Free card. The power of choice was liberating.

Paulo Coelho, who wrote the world famous *The Alchemist* says ...

'There is only one thing that makes a dream impossible to achieve:
the fear of failure.'

I believe that my dream was made possible because I focussed on success and its possibilities. If I had carried a fear of failure with me, that's what I would have achieved ... failure ... which would have been absolutely unthinkable and still is.

You may have asked this question of yourself: 'Is this all there is to my life?' Virginia Satir once said ...

'I become aware that this is the state of quiet desperation when nothing
really bad or really good happens. Life just goes on, day after day. You are
out of the overt conflict and left with the ceaseless yearning for something
better, but there is no energy available to act on it.'

And the questions continue: 'Is my life only going to amount to just okay, with ordinary interests and uninspiring friends?' 'Is my health and fitness mediocre?' There really is a better way. But if you just keep thinking about it, that is what you will get – just more thoughts. If you really want to take action, then just stop thinking about it and DO IT - *take action.* Make some real and concrete steps. Feel scared. Feel the fear and know it will be with you no matter what. Why not use it to give you energy and surprises, to take risks and get on with life? All this time you may have felt safe and kept yourself neatly tucked away from rejection and hurt. But are you feeling fear anyway? So, take control. Master your destiny like I have.

If you really want to take action, then just stop thinking about it and DO IT.

There have been so many rewards for me by doing this. I followed this formula long before the face cancer. For example, as a newly married woman many years ago, I received a United Nations Scholarship to travel to the United Kingdom. If I hadn't been encouraged to apply or thought I wasn't worthy or good looking enough, I wouldn't have followed through with an interview. And then my world wouldn't have opened up in the most amazing way that it did. This decision led to a new way of seeing the world. It also led to another opportunity, which was to be an ambassador on the State Council for Youth for two years. This led yet again to another world of challenge, excitement and growth.

My confidence grew, and then I was hit with the loss of my first baby at sixteen weeks into the pregnancy. I directed my devastation towards increasing my attention to my study and received the Council Medal at university, and this led to an opportunity to have input into the syllabus for new students in social work. I realised that some of my fears were great, but the next step, with the fear by my side, became a step to another step. Fear was always there. I used it like a manipulative child uses their parents. And so on it went.

Sometimes I have come to a crashing halt, but I am reinventing and growing all the time. I am now at an amazing time of my life, assisting people from all walks of life to deal with their fears, no matter who they are, and to embrace fear and get the life they want. Just thinking about it won't work. I assist people to take action, take risks and live with the fear. I feel excited by the prospects of all the amazing people I have met and will meet in the future, and the opportunities to create programs, write and spend more time with my family.

The skin cancer journey moved on, and after an accumulated twenty-five hours of surgery on my face and nose, I still have my nose. I am told that I could still lose it in the future and I am hanging onto it ever so tightly. I have come to adore the Japanese proverb:

'Fall down seven times, get up eight.'

This resonates so much with my view that life is a series of events, issues and problems that might knock you down, but no matter what, you keep getting up again. There is certainly always a choice. I choose to get up anytime a fearful situation presents itself and face it with courage, confidence and perseverance.

It's funny the things you remember when you look back. I clearly recall my loving older sister sitting next to my bed in hospital and, with a whole bunch of bandages on my face, she sneaked her finger up under the bandage ever so gently to see if I still had a nose. I was smiling inside. She thought I was still asleep from the effects of the anaesthetic, but I was wide awake. As her finger touched the edge of the bandage I said, 'It's OK. I still have my nose.' What a relief for us both.

The next piece of news was that I would probably lose my nose at some time in my life. Apparently, they decided to leave my nose right where it was with the acknowledged risk that it should really have been removed. I am so grateful to that doctor for taking that risk.

Fifteen years later, I still have a nose and it does all the things a good nose can do. It smells the ocean and the rain; it smells freshly baked bread and Thai food. It knows how to disperse the germs of a cold and gets itchy and annoying like any other good nose would do. And at times it can be very nosey. Yes, it's possible I will no longer have a nose in the future, and yet I see it as a challenge to create other choices, other dimensions to me that I never knew I had. I am already thinking that I could write a book if it happens while all my healing takes place. I could spend time with my gorgeous grandchildren, or I could simply sit and watch the satin bowerbird in my garden do its ritual mating dance. Anything is possible.

My life is truly extraordinary. I have the most amazing husband who is my best friend and always will be. Our lives are inextricably connected. We know each other's fears very well and move forward with this clear knowledge – but *we share the key as well.* And the bonus from this wonderful relationship is three beautiful daughters who have grown into the people I want to spend my time with. I am hoping that they can see how I moved ahead with my fear by my side and use that example to lead them through their own wonderful life journey. My vision for them, and for you, is to have a life full of hope, helpfulness, power, new possibilities, change and choice.

In the life that I lead, I am sharing the key of courage, confidence and perseverance. It is within you, also. Open the door and walk out and have a look around. You will be amazed.

Suggestions to Help You Live Extraordinarily by Taking Charge of Your Life With Fear by Your Side

❋ *Imagine the possibilities and take action*

Have you ever tried to imagine what your life would be like if you knew you could handle whatever life had to offer? Ask this question of yourself and let the answer(s) be your compass: ***What would I attempt or endeavour to do if I had the courage?*** You will never need courage while you watch TV, think, worry and procrastinate. Courage comes along when you take action – it feels surprisingly good.

❋ *Stop analysing your fear*

Stop wondering what is happening with your fear, where it has come from and how to get rid of it. By doing so you will free up space to focus on all the other things you want to achieve in your life. It really doesn't matter what causes your fear. All that matters is that you can trust yourself to take action and that you can handle whatever comes your way. Imagine that for a moment.

❋ *Do the very thing that you want to do but you are afraid to do*

The real deal is that this is the only way to get rid of your fear. The 'doing' is what actually causes the fear to go away. Everyone is wired the same way with fear so it's not about whether you have fear, it's what you do with it that counts. You can hold it up from a position of empowerment and with that comes tremendous choice. Give yourself permission to be strong, go forth with wonderment about your future and observe whether you are choosing to respond with fear or choice. Here are some little things that will help you to move forward: *smile more, say yes more, make more decisions, help others more, listen more and learn something new.* To your empowerment!

GET YOUR EXTRAORDINARY
FREE GIFT BONUS

Cath Edwards is kindly offering a **FREE BONUS GIFT**
to all readers of this book.

7 Steps to Magnifying your Success Formula and Conquering your Fears

An eBook to assist you to conquer fear,
regain energy and live a life of fulfilment.

Simply visit the web page below and follow the directions
to directly download *7 Steps to Magnifying your Success
Formula and Conquering your Fears.*

www.yesyoucancoaching.com

'... to make deep-seated change in your life
and change your unconscious beliefs,
you are best to bypass the ego
and deal with the unconscious mind.'

Sue Crosbie

Sue Crosbie is the founder and director of Spirited Woman Coaching, based in picturesque Katoomba in the Blue Mountain, New South Wales, Australia. Sue believes that having a spinal injury at the tender age of eighteen has given her a very different perspective on life. According to Sue, understanding her inner strengths and abilities when so young helped her to achieve so much more. In her words, 'I probably would have drifted around doing nothing for a very long time.'

While not really knowing what the big picture was, Sue always wanted to be moving forward and doing something new. So, now she is a self-confessed mid-life crisis addict (she's been through about five already) and she loves it! While deciding who she wanted to be when she grew up, Sue went from the corporate world to being a self-employed beauty therapist to working with disabled adults. She went to university at thirty years of age to complete an Economics degree, majoring in Psychology, to enter into the health system in Sydney. Now she uses that breadth of experience, combined with Neuro Linguistic Programming (NLP) and Hypnotherapy, to coach small to medium business owners to build successful businesses.

During the course of her own life discoveries, Sue has seen the needs of others when struggling with their past, their self-confidence and their limited beliefs in their own abilities. With her ever compassionate nature always wanting to help everyone, the burning question for her was, 'How can I help the most people to grow easily and effectively?' and to this end she has developed a series of audio tools to help her clients release negative emotions from the past and build a healthy and creative future. So everyone can get on with the fun stuff!

Be Responsible
for Your Outcomes
Who am I?

SUE CROSBIE

Hi. My name is Sue Crosbie, and I can say that so far I have led a very interesting life. Like most people, I've had my ups and downs, the usual dramas that we all go through – and some not so usual. But for me, what makes it interesting is how much I have learnt and grown from those life lessons.

Life was pretty idyllic up to the age of eighteen. I had loving parents raising my three brothers and myself. We lived on a 10-acre block of land just outside the small city of Invercargill at the bottom of New Zealand. Holidays were spent around the South Island nearly every long weekend and for two weeks every summer in our caravan at Lake Wanaka with our grandparents or cousins. You really don't get a better childhood. I think I was just cruising, with no real aim in life other than a desire to travel. I left school at sixteen just because I thought school sucked and I wanted to make some money (my older brothers hadn't really given me a good impression of school before I started).

At eighteen, however, everything changed. I was still in my first job working for Telecom NZ when I had to go out to one of the country shops to set up a phone display. My boss said, 'Drive safely,' which were fateful words because I then proceeded to roll the car up a hill – yes, up! I do like to be different. When the car finally stopped rolling, I thought, *I'll just walk to the petrol station down the road and ring my boss – he's not going to be happy with me!* But when I went to move, nothing happened. All I could think was that I might be there for a long time before someone found me. I saw blood dripping onto my skirt, but couldn't identify where it was coming from. I had visions of my arm being broken or crushed through my ribs – and my neck hurt!

Fortunately, people at the petrol station heard the crash and came straight up. I was in a little town called Dipton and my mum's best friend from high school lived there with her family. Val and her husband are like an aunt and uncle to me, so I asked the guys from the petrol station to call Val and gave them the phone number.

'You mean Colin's wife?' they asked. (It's a very small town.)

'Yeah,' I replied. I didn't remember that he was running an engineering shop right next door to the garage, so they got him to come up, too. I can't tell you how much it meant to me to have someone I knew there with me, especially Colin who has a very funny sense of humour. So, we sat there waiting for the ambulance, cracking a few jokes. It was the ski season and all I thought was: *Well, that's okay. Paraplegics can still ski.* It didn't really cross my mind that I was in fact a quadriplegic because I could still move my right arm slightly. But I knew my neck was broken because of the funny downward position it was now in.

I knew my neck was broken because of the funny downward position it was now in.

When they pulled me out of the car and put me on the stretcher, I was still cracking jokes with Colin, telling him how much I liked chocolate! For the whole ambulance ride I felt like I was still in the sitting position and hoped I wouldn't feel that way for the rest of my life; it was a very bizarre feeling.

About an hour later, I was in the emergency department at Invercargill's Kew Hospital where Mum was waiting for me. Colin had called her at work. This was the only time I cried, seeing how worried and upset Mum was; you never want to cause your mum that sort of worry. They had to drill two holes in my skull to put my neck into traction, and that was the weirdest sensation because I could hear everything. My skull really did sound empty with all that noise going on inside. They seemed to drill forever. To me it sounded like they'd drilled in two inches, but they told me it was only millimetres. You can imagine the jokes that I got from my family and friends, you know, like they knew I was brainless and thick-skulled. But, the funniest one was about growing some flowerpots in the holes. The best part came when the doctor finally straightened my neck and I felt like I was lying flat again; that was a relief.

So the upshot was one broken bone, C5/6, in the spinal cord – it was the only bone I had ever broken. Oh, and the blood. That was really funny because I only had the smallest cut on my finger, about a centimetre long. Later that night, I could feel tingling in my feet. I think maybe that was the point where I began to think I would walk away from this accident.

Discovering Inner Strength

The next day, Saturday, I was flown in a very small plane to the spinal unit at Burwood Hospital in Christchurch. It was an extremely uncomfortable flight where I would wake up feeling sick and the nurse would pump my stomach so I didn't vomit. Then she would pump me full of morphine. That happened several times. On the Sunday morning, I woke up to find my three older brothers had flown in from Australia where they were all living at the time. Mum and Dad had driven the seven hours to be with me, too.

The whole family were around my bed when the doctors told us that I would be in hospital for six months, was not likely to walk out of the hospital, and, if I did, I wouldn't get my bladder control back. All I saw was a vision of me at the beach in a bikini with a catheter and bag strapped to my leg. So, as you do when you're eighteen, I told them to get stuffed! I knew I would be walking home in time for Christmas.

Recovery involved a lot of hard work. I was in traction for six weeks. During this time, the physios would come daily and move my arms and legs around. The bed had to be tilted from side to side to prevent pressure areas, so they used pillows and sandbags to hold me in place. They couldn't wash my hair for the whole six weeks – very distressing for an eighteen year old and very itchy!

By the end of those six weeks, my body just wanted to sleep all the time and I had a lot of trouble staying awake for visitors. It seemed that everyone I knew in Invercargill had a relative in Christchurch and they all got them to come and visit me. Mum and Dad's bridesmaid and husband lived there, too, and either one or the other, or sometimes both of them, came to visit me every single day that I was in hospital. My bed was surrounded with cards, flowers and soft toys.

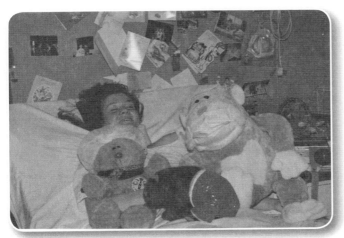

Sue in hospital after the accident.

One of my brothers even stayed in Christchurch for the whole time I was there. He got a job working on a building site in the city and stayed in the family section of the nurses' quarters. As a very good-looking lad, I think he had rather a good time with the nurses – especially as he ended up marrying one of them! I was incredibly well-supported by all my family and friends. The only one who didn't cope was my boyfriend, and I ended up breaking up with him the day after my nineteenth birthday party, which I had in hospital. That was tough emotionally, but one of the beautiful nurses took me outside to cry and talk it out.

When they finally took me off traction and sat me up in bed, I could only stay that way for half an hour before I got very dizzy and had to lie down again. So, it took a while to get me out of bed and into a wheelchair. After traction, the doctors decided I still needed to have surgery on my neck, so they performed an anterior fusion of my spine. That meant another six weeks with a neck brace on. Every day was a routine of working out with the physios and occupational therapists. Standing and walking between the parallel bars was very exciting, but, again, I couldn't do it for very long before I got dizzy. It was a long, slow process that required a lot of hard work and determination. But I did it.

Four months later, two days before Christmas, I walked down the stairs of the plane at Invercargill Airport. I think half of Invercargill had turned up to see me. I was using two walking sticks, but I was walking – and I had bladder control to boot! Okay, it was a bit like a pregnant woman's bladder; but hey, no catheter! And to me that was all that mattered.

That was twenty-five years ago. I still walk with a limp and my left hand doesn't open properly, so no running and none of the many sports I used to play. I'm pretty much over the gym, but it's one of the few ways I can stay fit, so I do go. I think the biggest thing that I still deal with on a daily basis now is how tired I get. Every step needs a higher level of concentration so I don't trip over my own toes, and that still happens sometimes. That level of concentration really does take it out of me.

There were benefits to my situation, too, the biggest being that I learnt really young what I had on the inside; an inner strength, courage and determination to do whatever I put my mind to. I know that I can do anything I want with this life as long as I want it enough. I've discovered a whole lot of tools to help me get there, and I really want to share some of these with you. If I can teach you how to believe in your own abilities, how to access your own inner strength, then I will feel like I've been truly useful. I can assure you, there is nothing special about me other than some of the knowledge I have gained, and I'm about to share that with you now, anyway.

I don't know why my response to the doctors had been to tell them to get stuffed. Whether I just couldn't see any other outcome, or if somewhere deep inside I knew that the tingling in my feet, or some other long-forgotten sign, indicated that the damage was not severe enough to stop me walking. Or perhaps it was to do with something that I now understand, and that is that completely believing that I would walk away from it was the most important part of my recovery.

What I didn't understand back then was that believing I would make a full recovery, right down

Believing I would make a full recovery, right down to visualising that as the only possible outcome, led me to manifest that outcome.

to visualising that as the only possible outcome, led me to manifest that outcome. I know that sounds like a bit of hocus-pocus, but it really isn't.

As long as your mind is working against you,
having what you want in life will be an uphill battle
– with yourself. Everything you need is on the inside.
Once you get your mindset right, you truly can do anything.

Taking Responsibility

So, how do you access the strength you have on the inside? The first step is to accept responsibility for you. This is the toughest step for most people. Once you can do this, you can do anything and the world will go out of its way to prove it to you! Don't believe me? Let me show you how it works.

How many people do you know who blame their life now on their parents, their childhood, a teacher, friends … (add your own person to blame here)? Okay, I can hear you saying, 'Yes but you had an idyllic childhood; you said so yourself. And I had … (such-and-such) … happen to me.'

Yes, you're right; I did have a fantastic childhood. But do you think I appreciated that as a teenager? Trust me. I was able to blame my parents for lots of things, just like most teenagers.

What about when I broke my neck? Don't you think that was big enough for me to use as an excuse not to be responsible for my outcomes for the rest of my life? I could have blamed my spinal injury for every failure since! I suppose I'm lucky; I always accepted responsibility for the car accident. I was mostly just grateful that I hadn't injured anyone else. I always thought that burden would have been difficult to live with. But I could still easily have used it as an excuse not to do many things.

At some point in my mid-twenties, I think about the time I became a mother myself, I started to appreciate my childhood. Before that, I hadn't actually understood just how lucky I had been. It took a mental process of forgiving my parents for their perceived wrongs to be able to then take responsibility for myself from that point forward. And then I began to fully appreciate my childhood. This is a process you must go through to really move forward in your life, even if you had the best parents or the worst. It's just the process of cutting the apron strings, which we all need to do at some point to grow up and be responsible for ourselves.

I don't mean to minimise the experiences anyone has been through: the traumas that many people face at many stages of life; the mental and physical abuses that people have to deal with; death of parents at a young age; the list is endless. The point here is that you can blame those events and be the helpless victim to them for the rest of your life or you can choose to take responsibility for your life from today and decide what your future will hold for you from a completely new perspective.

You are not responsible for what happened to you in the past, but you are certainly responsible for what happens to you from this point forward.

Accepting responsibility gives you the gift of choice. When you are able to see that you have options, the possibilities are endless.

Let me show you how it works. When I had my car accident I could easily have gone into blaming mode. I could have blamed my boss for sending me out on the road. I could have blamed the work car they had provided me, telling myself it wasn't suitable for country driving. I could have blamed God, like so many people seem to do when things go wrong. I could have been angry or resentful about my situation. I could have been a victim to that car accident, fearful of ever getting into another car or driving one myself. Do you think that if I were in blaming mode that my mind would have been able to focus so completely on my recovery and walking out? No.

Thank goodness I chose my own outcomes, not those of the doctors!

Regardless of how I ended up there, whether it was someone else's fault or my own, I could have chosen not to accept responsibility for my own outcomes from that point forward. Maybe when the doctors told me that I wouldn't walk again, I could have said to myself, 'They're the doctors, they would know.' Do you think I would have had the same outcomes? I think I would not have worked so hard to get out of that wheelchair if I hadn't believed it – because it really was hard work. I also think I would have spent a lot of time in self-pity mode. I'm not saying I haven't had those moments, I certainly have. But I think I could have remained in that state had I believed the doctors' verdict. Thank goodness I chose my own outcomes, not those of the doctors!

The simple act of taking responsibility for my future meant that my mind was focused on looking for ways to achieve those outcomes – like working really hard in the gym. This simple act of taking responsibility leads you to ask different questions of yourself. Instead of 'Why me?' you start asking yourself 'What do I want to change?' and 'How can I make that happen?'

When you get to that point, several things start to happen, and this is the bit where the universe starts to go out of its way to help you – or so it seems. There is a simple and logical explanation as to why this happens. It's called 'perception'. You see, once you ask your brain a question, like any computer it will start to look for an answer. So, while you are asking the 'Why me?' question, your brain is looking for the answer to that. If I had been asking the 'Why me?' question, I would have been looking for answers as to why I had to have that car accident. But because I was asking the 'What outcome do I want here?' and the 'How can I make that happen?' questions, my computer brain sought completely different answers.

When you change the question, not only do the answers change, but what you notice around you seems completely different, too. Your perception changes. Do you remember having a change in hairstyle? Maybe you went from long hair to a bob. Before you had your hair cut you might never have noticed anyone with a bob. But after your haircut and you walked away from the salon, you probably saw bobs everywhere. It's not that other people suddenly got their hair cut, too. It's because you can now perceive/see that hairstyle, whereas before you weren't noticing it. Nothing changed except your perception. (If you are a guy reading this and you don't know what a bob is, just replace it with 'your new car' and you're then noticing the same car everywhere – and you had thought it was so cool and original!)

That was how my mind was working, too. It was looking internally for memories and experiences that supported my being able to walk. So, I latched onto the tingling feeling in my toes as evidence that there was feeling there. It was also looking for external cues like 'How can I walk again? Well, work hard with the physios and do what they tell you to do.'

The world is full of opportunities if only we notice them.
Noticing the opportunities is the first step.
Acting on them is the second step.
Nothing will change if you don't take action.

Taking Action

This is the point where many people fail. I see it time and time again when I am coaching. While my clients understand the concept in theory, actually having to do something about it is where it all gets too hard and the myriad of excuses comes into play.

When I started university as a mature-age student, I started out with the intention of becoming a psychologist. During my first year, I had a friend who was going through 'issues' and I spent a lot of time on the phone trying to help her through them. What I soon realised was that she had no intention of changing – she just wanted someone to listen to her complaints and help her justify her stories. I realised she was not alone and I had to reconsider if that was the future career I wanted – listening to people complaining about their miserable lives. At the end of the first year, I transferred to an economics degree!

I chose business coaching over life coaching for the same reason. Anyone who has made the effort to start their own business is already an action taker and therefore more likely to take action to make change. What I have discovered along the way is that to successfully coach people in business, you first need to work through their values, beliefs and personal issues because these are the things that are holding them back in their business.

We all have beliefs that we develop over our lives, but most of these are formed before the age of seven.

So, how are our beliefs formed? We all have beliefs that we develop over our lives, but most of these are formed before the age of seven. We go through an event and attach a belief(s) to that event about ourselves, about others or how the world operates in general. We call this a defining moment. The beliefs we attach can be positive, supportive and nurturing, or negative and destructive. The events can be significant or small. One of my beliefs was that I was an ugly child with crooked teeth, freckles and hair that stuck out. This belief was formed on the playground when I was about six years old. I was chasing a boy I liked, Stephen, and he told me I was ugly and ran away from me. That was the event where I formed the belief I was ugly – it was a defining moment.

What happens next in this sort of scenario is called the Law of Congruency. We need to feel congruent with our beliefs, so we look for evidence that what we believe is true. So, like the haircut, we start to notice the evidence that supports our belief. I would see the ugly in the mirror, not the pretty. I would remember the man who found me playing in our driveway dressed in overalls and gumboots and asked, 'Where is your father, sonny?' These are the events I remember, not the ones where I might have been in a pretty dress and received a compliment. The problem is that, as adults, we generally don't remember attaching the belief to the original event. Then we have no idea that in our current life we are filtering in things to support a notion developed in childhood.

You can see my photo and decide for yourself if you think I'm pretty or ugly, as beauty is in the eye of the beholder. To change my belief about my beauty or non-beauty, I went through a process of recognising the belief, then changing the belief and the emotional energy that I had attached to that very first event. From an adult's perspective, I now understand that as a six year old Stephen probably thought all girls had 'girl germs'. I also chose to believe I am like a good red wine that gets better with age; I have grown out of my ugly duckling childhood and become the swan. I looked back over the past and discovered the evidence that I had filtered out that had shown I was actually beautiful.

I now have a new belief and emotional energy around my looks. This has changed my confidence in myself as well. I can accept that I can look 'ho hum' when I get out of bed, knowing that a shower can work miracles! I have identified several other defining moments in my life that were good and some that were not so good, and I then went through this same process with the negative ones.

So, what are your defining moments and how are they affecting what you are filtering in about the world around you and creating negative self-beliefs?

To find your defining moments, think about an event of significance from your childhood, usually before the age of seven. Ask yourself what happened, how you felt and what you told yourself about how life works from that experience. Accept whatever memory pops into your mind as your unconscious mind has raised it for a reason.

Once you've pinpointed these beliefs, changing them is best done at the unconscious level of the mind – and I can show you how to transform these beliefs effortlessly. But first I need to explain a bit about how the mind works.

Once you've pinpointed these beliefs, changing them is best done at the unconscious level of the mind.

I define the mind as having two parts: your conscious mind or everything you are currently focused and aware of, often called the ego; and the unconscious mind, everything you are not currently focused on. It stores your memories, your past and your projections about the future.

Consider this. We have about two million bits of information hitting our senses every second and if we had to process all that information it would literally fry our brain. To deal with this, our brain adapts by filtering what information it takes in. We can consciously deal with about 134 bits of those 2 million bits and we chunk that into seven chunks (plus or minus two). *[This was worked out by some brilliant guy whose name I can't remember, but I don't want to take the credit from him.]* Everything else that is not one of the seven chunks we are currently thinking about is part of our unconscious. You are currently focussing on these words, but if I were to ask you where you are sitting or lying, you would suddenly become very aware of that, even though you probably weren't two seconds ago. It's not that you didn't know where you were sitting; it's just that it wasn't one of your seven chunks until I mentioned it.

If you and I are watching a live dance performance together, we will each have a very different experience of that show based on what we notice – your seven chunks might include more the colours in the costumes, the sets and story line, whereas my chunks may be more involved in the technique of the dancers, their expression and the lighting. What we filter in will be partially due to our past experiences, beliefs and knowledge. For example, as my daughter is a dancer and I have been watching her learn to dance for the last fourteen years, I will appreciate the technique so much more than I did in the past; hence, my experience of the show. These different experiences then create a map, in our brain, of that show. You may think it was wonderful with all the beautiful costuming and sets, whereas I may think it only ordinary as the standard of the dancing wasn't very good.

You can see now why all our maps are a bit different. Have you ever thought someone was a bit weird? Well, if you knew their maps, you would understand how they came to be that way and why it is all perfectly logical to them. This is why there is no reality, only our perception or map of reality.

So, the upshot of all this diagnosis of the mind, our brain maps and how it all works is that *to make deep-seated change in your life and change your unconscious beliefs, you are best to bypass the ego and deal with the unconscious mind.* That's like bypassing the secretary and getting straight to the boss. The easiest way to do that is through getting into the Theta brain wave state, as it opens a direct channel to the unconscious mind. Experienced meditators go into this state, as does a person under hypnosis.

The unconscious mind also likes to work using symbology. Remember your last dream and you will see your unconscious mind at its most active. The dream probably made no sense to you at the time, and that is because of the symbology. A metaphor is a form of symbology, and that is one reason why stories have so much impact on us. Of course, listening to a story is firstly much more enjoyable (and less challenging) than being told what to do, believe or change directly. But, secondly, the unconscious mind loves the symbology and understands the meanings much better than the conscious mind does, thereby creating change at a much deeper level of the mind. The conscious mind, or ego, may not understand the symbology as clearly and is then less resistant to the

The unconscious mind loves symbology and understands the meanings much better than the conscious mind does, thereby creating change at a much deeper level.

messages being offered – it's just enjoying the story! The use of metaphors also means that your unconscious mind will interpret the messages for you in a way that is congruent with your core values.

Another reason why using these techniques combined – getting into the Theta brain wave state and using symbology – makes the transformation process very easy is because you don't need to talk through all the issues as you would in a counselling session. What's the problem with this? When you go to a counsellor the standard form of therapy is to get you to discuss your problems. But what this does is create stronger neural pathways around 'the problem' – reinforcing them.

Conversely, by using meditation or hypnosis with suggestive metaphors, you are not building neural pathways around 'the problem'. You instead are gently releasing the emotional energy connected to 'the problem', without the need to talk about it. You release yourself from your negative stories and unhelpful limiting beliefs that were formed right back at the beginning in your defining moments. You are allowing your unconscious mind to make the shift, releasing old emotional attachments and creating new positive ones.

So, What is your Story and Are you Ready to Let it Go?

I challenge you to just stop talking about your story – let it go, especially if it is a major focus of your life.

You may find that you don't have much to talk about for a while, particularly if you have been very wrapped up in it until now. This does not only refer to the conversations we have with others, but also the conversations we have with ourselves inside our head!

We all have events that occur in our lives and my intention is not to have you believing you can avoid such situations. The real benefit comes from your strengthened ability to deal with those situations easily and quickly as they arise, with an inner confidence in yourself and your abilities.

I challenge you to just stop talking about your story – let it go, especially if it is a major focus of your life.

You may also find that if you have lived the archetype of Martyr or Drama Queen you will no longer need to fulfil your core needs of significance and connection through the drama. Ultimately, you will have less drama in your life as you develop new programs and new ways to fulfil these core needs.

I can truly say that in my life now I am much more self-deterministic about who I am and what I want out of life. I am much less fearful about having a go and will readily make the changes I need to, to go in the direction that I want. The best outcome I have gained so far has been creating the most wonderful relationship in my life after a couple of disasters, which meant having both the belief in my worth and the belief that there was someone out there with the same values and ability to love that I do. Not to mention the ability to love completely, without holding back because of past failures. I still have challenges (and tears), but feel very able to deal with them and get past them far more quickly. Being responsible for my outcomes and myself gives me the freedom to choose my own future based on values and beliefs that are supportive and beneficial.

It has taken me years to learn all this amazing knowledge and I have really crammed in as much as I could into this chapter so you can have the benefit of my years right now. So, take this information, use it, and see what radical changes you can make, too.

Suggestions to Help You Live Extraordinarily by Taking Responsibility Today for your Future Outcomes

Accept the past
Accept the past, learn whatever you need to learn from it and let the story go. You can change the meaning of the event any time you like because your perception of the event was created within your mind – so just give it new meaning.

Take responsibility for your thoughts and actions

When you are responsible for your thoughts and actions today, you create the ability to choose your outcomes for tomorrow. Practice by changing a limiting thought pattern or doing something creative that you would not have dreamed of doing before; prove to yourself you can do it.

 Make time for you

Make time for you, time to just sit and be still, time to allow your unconscious mind to understand, to heal and to discover the changes you need to make to create a life that fulfils YOU!

GET YOUR EXTRAORDINARY
FREE GIFT BONUS

Sue Crosbie is kindly offering a **FREE BONUS GIFT** to all readers of this book.

One month's access and download of the *Time for You* self-development audio series.

This is part of a simple-to-use audio series that can transform your life in just 15 minutes a day, helping you to make changes in your life the easy way.

Simply visit the web page below and follow the directions to directly download one month's access to *Time for You*.

www.timeforyouaudios.com

'Women generally are not very good at negotiating for themselves. The principle of 'Nice girls don't ask' can be seriously crippling to any life fulfilment. I have found that women often don't get what they want and deserve simply because they just don't ask for it.'

Bianca Carroll

Bianca Carroll is an Accredited Extended DISC consultant/trainer, Business and Leadership Strategist, and Life Coach based in New South Wales, Australia, working with people who are excited and driven towards designing their Destiny. Whether that's shaping the home, leading teams, optimising their sales or building their business, Bianca is excited to bring to life the success principles that generate results.

Having worked in both corporate and private sectors, Bianca has gained keen and unique insights from being in the front line of managing people, starting from the role of receptionist and advancing to branch manager.

Throughout her working career of over twenty-five years, Bianca has learnt that achieving great sales and business results requires much more than just the technical requirements – understanding people and how to work with them is pivotal to achieving results. And it's not just about financial results. 'Knowing people and how to give them what they want is so much more than that.' Bianca acknowledges the individual and the value they bring to the transaction and the organisation, and she assists them in attaining the goals they are aspiring to.

With her insight, Bianca provides a basis of empathy and a clearer strategy towards progression and fulfilment that is beyond the technical aspects of the business. To this end she utilises DISC (Dominance, Influence, Steadiness, Conscientiousness), which is a leading personal assessment tool for improving work productivity, teamwork and communication. Bianca works effectively with individuals, teams and organisations that are ready to make a change and unlock their full potential to achieve results.

Bianca is also a mother of two daughters who are embarking on their own paths and is happily married to the 'love of her life'. She has a fulfilling work-home balance and is happy to help any woman to create this magic within their own lives.

Finding Your Own Magnificence

From Duck to Swan

BIANCA CARROLL

How many times have you told yourself that you should be happy with your lot in life, or that things could be worse, or that you shouldn't rock the boat?

I would like to share my story and in doing so perhaps highlight the potential that you hold right now, which extends far beyond the title of 'Mum', 'Wife', 'Friend' and so on. It's essentially about claiming your title of 'Self' and permitting yourself to be exactly who you are. When you think about it, if you don't know who you are, then who will?

Before I Could Fly

Many years ago, I joined the workforce as a receptionist. Fresh from secretarial college and not even completing my final year in high school, I had set off to make my mark on the world. My thoughts at that time were to be a hard-working employee so that perhaps one day, after demonstrating years of dedication and enthusiasm, I might ascend to a sales role.

My boss at the time was happy if I would deliver his coffee, type up a few letters and memos, know the alphabet so I could retrieve and collate client files, empty his ashtray twice a day and fetch his lunch – job done! He never seemed to ask me for anything extra and he would often walk straight past my desk to ask the male trainee to attend client meetings with him. I guess I knew my place.

It wasn't long before I came to understand that there was more to what I was capable of and I developed an itching desire to want to achieve more. Yet I knew the current situation would never allow me to make my mark. The obstacle, I believed, was the male attitude and how I needed to adapt to manoeuvre around this.

Day after day my boss would pass by my desk to speak to the male trainee and reinforce those nagging doubts I had that I wasn't good enough to attend to clients or that all I'd be good for was fetching coffee and typing letters – after all that was what females did in the office.

I would often look at the other women in the office, all of whom seemed tired and overworked as they attended quietly to tidying up the loose ends that the manager had overlooked in his haste to meet up with other business managers. Oh, and their meeting place – a gentlemen's club.

Was this going to be my life in twenty years' time? Would this be enough to satisfy me? Perhaps I was better off starting that family and focusing on being the best mum I could be. Other women seemed to enjoy this and always spoke how it was their finest achievement.

Okay, so fast forward to 2005 (some twenty years later). I had two teenage daughters and had worked and lived in three different states, following my husband at the time in his career postings. We also purchased a business together. I thought I had it all – the balance every woman dreams of: great family life, thriving kids and an abundant career.

How mistaken I was. Within a few years, I had divorced my husband and sold my part of the business.

The great thing about hindsight is that we can rewind and replay events to find some key learning or message to ensure we are able to make more informed choices. My key learning at that time was to see that I had never believed that I was a decision maker in my life. Life just turned up and all I needed to do was to play along. Go with the flow, roll with the tide. It goes a little deeper than that as well for me. In all my roles, whether that was as wife, work colleague or business partner, I had always felt that I played second fiddle. I had

The great thing about hindsight is that we can rewind and replay events to find some key learning or message.

believed that the ultimate decision to proceed with something was not actually mine to make.

I still remember times when I was designated to deal with sales reps so that my husband was allowed time to focus on the 'real' running of the business. I would talk with the sales reps and even if I thought they might have something good to offer our business, I would always stop and say something like, 'Thanks for your time. I will have to run this past my manager. So, once I have his decision I will get back to you.'

The funny thing is that now I have female clients who say pretty much the same thing. 'Oh, my husband understands those things.' Or 'That's too complicated for me. Are you able to write that down so I can show my husband?' I always smile and think their day will come, and hopefully as you read on you too can believe that your day is almost here.

As my girls got older, I started to find my own voice, just a little bit at first. The roles of mother and business partner had suffocated me to such a point that I was slowly dying inside. But something inside me wanted to fight back, to breathe. I remembered my commitment to myself those twenty or so years earlier that I wanted to make my mark on the world. Heck, don't I deserve that?

Stretching my Wings

So, I began to openly express my opinion, which usually meant the opposite to my husband's. I started to embrace who I am and to see myself as equal to my husband, who was also the managing director of the business. Of course, the guilt I had at times was palpable – how dare I?

I experienced an internal conflict between my obligations (which others assumed that I actually wanted) and the direction I wanted to head towards where I knew I would feel alive. I chose to follow the direction of empowerment of my-self. I had been trained to stay in my box long enough.

As a result of my expressing my capabilities in making multiple decisions and multi-tasking (taking on a more masculine persona), my husband, on some level, no longer needed to be the provider. And through my new expression of self, my determination and following through, I believe he lost his sense of purpose at that time. Without elaborating on the details, we decided to dissolve our marriage.

Now before I continue, I must express to you that I had no knowledge at the time of what I'm about to share with you about human behaviours, amongst other things. Remember, I was still going with the flow to some degree. Further, while this is my story, it doesn't need to be yours, and you don't need to feel like you have to sacrifice anything in order to be all of who you are – a balance is totally achievable.

In 2007 I became a branch manager for a corporate insurance broker, I re-married, and today I am a business and leadership consultant in the Central West of NSW, Australia. I work to empower other women who have found that leadership is one skill amongst their many abilities. You see, I dug deep to find the gold, and now with courage and certainty of self I can share not only my story but also assist others to find their own path.

Now, how I got to where I am now sounded way too easy. Let me break this down so you can see what was really going on for me and how I got to this point.

When I applied for the branch manager position, I felt totally out of my depth. The company had actually posted two positions: one as branch manager and the other as an account executive. I knew I would easily slip into the account executive role, but doubted that I had what it took to step up as an actual manager. With those doubts, I realised I was starting to go back to my old pattern of self-doubt, playing a victim and throwing in the towel – It's all too hard. But I had worked so hard to get to this point; was I about to fold now?

So far in life I had mastered playing it safe, and I remember sitting on my bed saying to myself something like, Well, Bianca. Is continuing like this going to be enough for you? Are you going to play the 'safe' game again? I projected my mind forward and knew that deep down I would be kicking myself for at least not trying. What's the worst that can happen after all?

I agonised for over three weeks before I finally submitted my application. When I eventually hit the send button on the email, I leapt around the room like a crazy woman asking, 'What have I done?' I again had to give myself another severe talking to in order to squelch the fear bubbling up and those nagging questions: What if I get an interview? What if they ask me things I don't have answers for? Ok, time to find that red wine!

Now what I should elaborate on here is that in my mind I had built up an impression of what it takes to be a branch manager. I'd made this so big in my mind that it was insurmountable. I thought to sit in the manager's chair you needed to be the best of the best. You would have knowledge beyond that of the team, be excellent with figures, budgeting, marketing and people – knowing their strengths and weaknesses and how to motivate them towards the business objectives. Further, managers had to have great self-awareness, remain calm under pressure, be able to facilitate and negotiate difficult situations, and still be able to sleep at night knowing they have imparted their wisdom and served the greater good!

I merely thought my interview was a way of ensuring they met their fair and equal opportunity requirements to demonstrate they included women in their interview process.

I went from one end of the scale to the other in my head – one minute being totally confident, the next a blithering idiot filled with self-doubt. Who was I after all? A divorcee who once owned a share in a business – ditto. Even in my interview I attempted to talk my soon-to-be manager out of employing me as I had already perceived that the person they wanted for this job was a male business type leader that would run the branch and motivate the team to bring in the results. I merely thought my interview was a way of ensuring they met their fair and equal opportunity requirements to demonstrate they included women in their interview process.

To my surprise, though, not only did they employ me, but they offered me the job within three hours of the interview. Clearly they were more convinced of my abilities than I was! It had happened! Finally! I can't tell you what a relief it was to have had that recognition; to know that I was actually worthy. I wasn't crazy after all!

So, there I was in my new role; the first female regional branch manager in this organisation's history. In my view, it was a monumental change on some level for the organisation; however, it appeared to go by relatively unnoticed.

As each day passed, I realised this wasn't going to be as tough as I had imagined. Have you ever lain in bed when the room is dark and start seeing dark shadows moving? It was almost like that. I had been jumping at shadows all this time, but I now knew I was only skimming the surface of my abilities as a leader.

I discovered within a week that everything I had thought you needed in order to be a manager I already had in abundance. True, some skills were still in their infancy, but I knew these were growth and development opportunities. The other surprise was that I realised that all managers are doing the best they can with the knowledge they have at the time, and most of them have been elected to head a team by default, without any real leadership training.

How could I have thought such a role beyond me and only those who were really brilliant should hold such a position? How did I believe that I was not worthy?

Too often women see themselves as less capable of completing a task when the reality is they are more than capable.

The bonus lesson I learnt is that too often women see themselves as less capable of completing a task when the reality is they are more than capable. The flipside of that is often a male counterpart can see certain tasks actually beneath their ability when in reality they are less capable of completing the task competently. Basically, women will apply for jobs when they think they can do them, while men will apply for jobs they want to do.

Women generally are not very good at negotiating for themselves. The principle of 'Nice girls don't ask' can be seriously crippling to any life fulfilment. I have found that women often don't get what they want and deserve simply because they just don't ask for it.

Why do you think this is? … Fear? Fear of what exactly? Perhaps fear that if you do something different and it doesn't work you will look foolish.

Fear can hold you back, yet fear can also propel you forward depending on your perspective. I managed to turn my fear into a propulsion mechanism, and as I faced my fears I learnt that the biggest fear I had was to reach seventy without having tried; that my opportunity to be that role model for my children, self and others would have passed me by, and worse, that I would have allowed it! To me, that would be the ultimate disappointment – a life not lived.

Taking Flight and Soaring Above

In the areas of our business and personal relationships, our roles as women have changed dramatically. There is nothing that we can't achieve, and in some ways we should empathise with the males in not knowing what their role is anymore.

Women for the most part want the males in their lives to be able to lead, and by that we have evolved to understand it is not leading through control or domination. In fact the woman is looking for a man who, through strength and steadfastness, will support her efforts and encourage her, rather than be intimidated by her courage.

As David Deida puts it in his book, *The Way of the Superior Man:*

'Women are the ocean, wild, often unpredictable and prone to changing their minds in 5 minutes, if not every 5 minutes. Men are the ship that sails over the ocean, directional, purposeful and strong.'

Many of us women are concerned that by stepping up and following through on our desires we may leave our male counterparts behind. And what if we outgrow our male leader/partners altogether? How do we respect our own passions and desires while respectfully acknowledging theirs?

It's important for the male to be able to lead, just not for the ransom of taking away the desires of the woman. Perhaps I should elaborate a little more on what male and female energy is – give you some definitions to put some clarity around this.

FEMININE ENERGY

- Focuses on people
- Home spirited
- Sensual and open
- Creates space for emotions
- Enjoys being connected with people
- Seeks love
- Enjoys working towards a common goal
- To fully live in the present moment
- Passive
- Submissive
- Yielding

MASCULINE ENERGY

- Focuses on facts
- Individualistic
- Solution-orientated
- Disciplined
- Plans and organises
- Seeks freedom
- Enjoys control and leadership
- To follow a life purpose
- Aggressive
- Dominant
- Directional

Above is a quick snapshot of the different aspects of feminine and masculine energies. Please remember as you read this that the list is not gender-specific. We all have male and female energies within us and the task at hand will determine which energy we might choose to get the task done. Also, this chapter is merely an introduction to this topic. We can't cover the whole spectrum here, and Ghania Dib will cover it a little more for you with her Key.

Note that there are mature and immature versions of each of these points. For example, the masculine energy enjoys control. An immature version of this could be a bully who is only after what they can gain, whereas a mature version of control would be to lead others through a situation, and show determination and strength at a time when others need it.

Someone that is predominantly male energy can come across as arrogant and too sure of themselves. Someone that is predominantly female energy can come across as too 'off with the fairies'.

Interestingly, I feel that we are all seeking this balance, or dare I suggest – harmony – in life between the masculine and feminine energies within. Too much control and we feel overworked and undervalued. Too much relaxation and we feel we have no purpose and direction.

Whilst on the surface male and female appear to be the opposite of each other, they are actually counterparts to each other. This simply means that male cannot exist without female and vice-versa. There needs to be both yin and yang, male and female. Even our power adapters have prongs and slots.

In this new era of equality and opportunities for anyone willing to expand beyond their current reality, know that the male and female energies, when synergised correctly, can work together in harmony quite beautifully. This is after all how life is formed, and when we have this balance, this is when we can feel truly alive.

What I would like to elaborate on now are two aspects of femininity and masculinity that I have highlighted in the lists above:

> *Feminine*   ✿   *to fully live in the present moment*
> *Masculine*   ✿   *to follow a life purpose*

What I have come to learn from my own experience, and from other women around me, is that we have been lacking 'life purpose'. We plugged that 'purpose' with things such as motherhood, busying ourselves with the cleanest house in the street or providing the best cupcakes for our kid's parties.

Do these things drive you towards a compelling and exciting future? Do they put the juice in your tank? If so, awesome stuff and congratulations. However, let me ask:

> *What happens when the kids have left home*
> *and can make their own decisions?*

> *What happens when someone comes into the house*
> *with mud on their shoes?*

> *What happens when someone else's cupcakes are better?*

My mother and other women of similar age often comment how life was different for them 'back in their day'. They elaborate that if they had had the opportunities available to them that we now have, their lives would have taken different directions. These women felt their role was to look after the children and support their male, and through their male's ascension and realisation of his goals somehow they (women) would be satisfied. Remember the saying, 'Behind every great man is a great woman'? What a great way to reinforce what their role was.

The 50's was also the height of the baby boom years where women were expected to stay at home as housewives and mothers. This expectation also reflected in the enrolments in secondary education. As we progressed, some women never budged from their duties as they were managed through fear and intimidation, often told that they would be unable to survive without the male. And the world at the time supported this belief.

You had role models such as Jackie Onassis and Lucille Ball. There was little support for single women, abused or not. Women often went straight from the family home and school into a marriage, to have children and repeat the cycle.

Well-paying jobs were only available to career men. Men were leaders in all facets of organisations and institutions. Schools, hospitals, churches and the corporate world perpetuated the belief that women should remain behind the scenes and find fulfilment in motherhood and being a servant to their male colleague/boss/partner.

We only need to look at movies and how the roles of women in movies have changed through the ages. Movies portrayed women as victims and men as heroes, generally speaking. Advertising, even in the 1950's, was pitched at how good you would be as a wife and mother if you used a certain product in your cooking, or used a certain makeup to make you more attractive for your husband.

You need not look further than the following excerpt from **The Good Wife's Guide** from **Housekeeping Monthly**, *13 May 1955*. This explains very clearly the place of a 'good wife', which was the primary concern for women of the day:

- *Have dinner ready. Plan ahead, even the night before, to have a delicious meal ready on time for his return. This is a way of letting him know that you have been thinking about him and are concerned about his needs. Most men are hungry when they get home and the prospect of a good meal is part of the warm welcome needed.*

- *Prepare yourself. Take 15 minutes to rest so you'll be refreshed when he arrives. Touch up your make-up, put a ribbon in your hair and be fresh-looking. He has just been with a lot of work-weary people.*

- *Be a little gay and a little more interesting for him. His boring day may need a lift and one of your duties is to provide it.*

- *Clear away the clutter. Make one last trip through the main part of the house just before your husband arrives. Run a dust cloth over the tables.*

- *Greet him with a warm smile and show sincerity in your desire to please him.*

- *During the cooler months of the year you should prepare and light a fire for him to unwind by. Your husband will feel he has reached a haven of rest and order, and it will give you a lift too. After all, catering to his comfort will provide you with immense personal satisfaction.*

- *Listen to him. You may have a dozen important things to tell him, but the moment of his arrival is not the time. Let him talk first – remember, his topics of conversation are more important than yours.*

- *Don't greet him with complaints and problems.*

- *Don't complain if he's late for dinner or even if he stays out all night. Count this as minor compared to what he might have gone through at work.*

- *Make him comfortable. Have him lean back in a comfortable chair or lie him down in the bedroom. Have a cool or warm drink ready for him.*

- *Arrange his pillow and offer to take off his shoes. Speak in a low, soothing and pleasant voice.*

- *Don't ask him questions about his actions or question his judgment or integrity. Remember, he is the master of the house and as such will always exercise his will with fairness and truthfulness. You have no right to question him.*

- *A good wife always knows her place.*

I hope that as you read through this you truly appreciated just how far we have come. Women at this time did believe this was all they were capable of, and why not when media was pitched to support this belief. They further believed the key to a fulfilling life was to serve others.

Do you think women wanted to do more than be a wife and maintain a home? Perhaps do things like, say, become a pilot? Or a doctor? Absolutely they did and still do. There were of course acceptable roles such as being a stewardess or a nurse that women settled for as those fitted in nicely with the traditional role of 'support' person.

What about certain television shows I grew up with – *The Brady Bunch, Bewitched, I Dream of Jeannie?* Do you remember the roles the main female character and the male character had? It is little wonder that we, both male and females, are confused after years of conditioning with this type of stereotyping. Has the world really changed so much since then or have we just become aware and acknowledged our own desires? What if on some level we are merely seeing the evidence that has always been there and through our new self-awareness our focus is shifting? Previously it was just dismissed or perceived as unimportant. Or maybe we were distracted, seeking evidence to support our limits, such as how we got passed over for a certain job, or how it's only 'me' that has to stay home when the kids are sick, or that 'I' will never be able to be a leader of a team.

I remember when I had a major shift in awareness. One of my male managers would often stay at work longer than he needed to in order to make sure when he got home the kids were all bathed, fed, in bed and his dinner in the oven. He even joined Apex and the Chamber of Commerce in order to have legitimate meetings after work. But, like him his wife had a full time job at the time. She would take her lunch hour at 3.15 pm in order to grab the kids and drop them off to afternoon care.

For me, the moment I learnt of the details of this relationship is frozen in time – It was my awakening. It was at that point that I clearly understood that I was truly more than a mum and a wife. That frozen snapshot of time that I glimpsed through the looking glass became my motivator. I knew then that only I had the power to make life what I wanted it to be, and if I wanted to settle for less and roll-over-Rover, it would mean that that version of reality I was looking at would be mine, also. Yes, this very well could have been my story.

Being a mum is merely a vehicle to fulfilling your core needs on a basic human level. So is being a gardener, or a volunteer, or a career woman. The trick is to ensure these vehicles are hitting the target in positive, sustainable and resourceful ways.

If your current reality is not satisfying you, you can live a life that is abundant beyond your current reality; more compelling and exciting than you could ever have imagined. Something that fills you up on the inside, to the point of bursting.

Holding ourselves back will only lead to the inner turmoil and self-talk to ensure that we never progress and fulfil our dreams and potential. Remember my own drama when I pushed past the pain barrier to apply for the branch manager's role?

The thing to understand here is that people will do more to avoid pain than to gain pleasure. I had to reach my threshold, which was when the pain of staying the same became greater than the pain of the unknown.

Whether your desire is to return to work, put your hand up for a promotion, change jobs, volunteer, or simply do something for yourself guilt free, remember that the only difference between dreams and goals is action. You can set up a different future if you so desire.

It should be easy, shouldn't it? To jump right out there and start doing something for you?

Well, if change was that easy you would have done it already, right? If you are anything like me, I can imagine the concerns you have right now around changing.

Let's be realistic. To traverse onto your pathway, especially if you've been hidden within a false sense of purpose for so long, you are likely to face strong objections. Objections from partners, family, friends … and most of all, yourself.

Things like: My husband won't like it. How will this affect my relationship? What will the kids do if I do XYZ? What will my parents think of me? What if I love it? What if I fail? My sister is so not going to accept this. Last time I attempted doing XYZ it caused a huge rift … all the ripple effects that you might cause. The list is endless.

If you do have thoughts like those going around and around in your head, it's again another reason to know that something does need to change. It may not even be the thing you are thinking of either!

New Horizons

In case you haven't guessed what my passions are and what truly lights me up, it's the opportunity to work with women, just like you, that are perhaps stuck or at a cross-roads; to assist them to access their potential that has been bubbling away below the surface for too long.

I have seen women blossom and come to life as they take those steps in claiming their path. There is nothing more beautiful when a woman is in harmony with herself, and when this occurs, the abundant joy she has is a magnet to others. I appreciate those first steps to changing can be unfamiliar. Even if only one aspect of life were to change, it could be enough to bring you better results than you are currently experiencing.

Bianca in Venice. A time when she realised her potential was limitless.

Women often want to share their joy – part of their nurturing essence – and their family and friends will also reap the benefits. I mean, who would you rather be around, someone that is constantly complaining, nit-picking and nagging, or someone that is at peace, exuding brilliant happiness and achieving their desires?

It's often said that the definition of insanity is to keep doing the same things but expecting different results. So, if you are feeling stuck on that treadmill and spinning your wheels, you might be ready to try something new.

- *Have you felt that there needs to be more to life but you're not sure exactly what?*
- *Have you got a great business idea and not sure how to put it together?*
- *Have you got an untapped skill?*
- *Have you thought of returning to work or changing jobs?*

For every person that has ever said something is 'impossible' there is always another person proving that theory wrong. For example, the world is flat, the speed of sound cannot be broken, a phone cannot fit in your pocket and so forth. When we learn to question what we perceive on face value and shift our perception slightly, we can often discover something that was always evident, just no-one was looking for it.

Have you ever been told you can't do something and then achieved it? Only you will define your limits or allow others to limit you.

Did you know that the invention of the light bulb took at least 3,000 'failures' before there was something that resembles what we have today? Did this deter the inventors? Thomas Edison merely stated, 'We now know a thousand ways not to build a light bulb'. It's an encouraging thought – by having those 'failures' they narrowed down their options, thus increasing the possibilities of achievement.

Your Swan Song

Okay, you've made it to this point, and I'm imagining that you are itching to make a move. This is your time to Design your Destiny and create your own Swan Song.

Along the way, you may be met with objections from others, and even worse, your own limiting self-talk. As you can see from the light bulb scenario, the road to brilliance is to keep on going till you get it right. Just as Thomas Edison didn't allow a seemingly never ending amount of objections stop him from his dream of creating light for where there is dark, nor should you be deterred from sparking your own darkness until it is whole and bright.

My parting words to you are:

- *We all have the potential to be, to do and to have anything we want. It only depends on our level of focus to its attainment.*

- *Know that you are more than capable of achievement and that you deserve an extraordinary life.*

- *Embrace all of who you are and know there is no-one quite like you. You are magnificently you.*

Suggestions to Help You Live Extraordinarily by Believing you are Capable of Being More if you Want to Be

Uncover and develop your skills and abilities

The lives of others lost in daily longings for more than what they've achieved should remind us not to lose our own aspirations. The world is full of powerful, capable people who have never discovered their inner power and full capabilities. If you feel you are underachieving and not living your full potential, make the commitment to yourself to find out where uncovering old skills and developing new abilities will take you. Know that full potential does exist – in you. Find out what it's like to live in potential rather than without.

Trust you have all you need to be all that you want to be

Develop trust in yourself that you do have the abilities to be all that you want to be. Though these abilities may have previously been masked by doubt and fear – remember my doubts that I could ever be a leader – trust that you have it within you to take on any challenge and be anything you wish to be. Trust becomes confidence, a true inner confidence devoid of arrogance, that will enable you to act on any challenge.

Use mantras and affirmations

Any limits placed on you are placed there by your own self, even though it often appears as if these limitations and constrictions are placed on us by others and by circumstance. Repeat a mantra to yourself often, making it your own private ritual. Find words to express to yourself that limitlessness is your reality. Try this: I have absolutely no limitations on what I intend for my life.

GET YOUR EXTRAORDINARY
FREE GIFT BONUS

Bianca Carroll is kindly offering a **FREE BONUS GIFT** to all readers of this book.

Pathways to Power

A walk-through guide that includes a worksheet on identifying the areas you want to improve, how to map and track your goals, as well as a guide to handling objections from others and identifying limiting self-talk – an informative yet simple tool to help you put together your own blueprint for moving forward.

Simply visit the web page below and follow the directions to directly download *Pathways to Power*.

www.biancacarrollconsulting.com

'Whatever new beliefs you choose,
just start LIVING. Choose TODAY to be
a greater version of YOU and LIVE a life of
Energy, Vitality and Purpose!'

Minda Lennon

Minda Lennon is a Wellness Coach based in the Sunshine Coast, Australia. She is also a certified Personal Trainer, Life Coach, Neuro Linguistic Practitioner, Matrix Therapist and Trainer, and a consultant of Extended DISC (Behavioural Profiling). She applies evidence-based techniques from coaching psychology and positive psychology to assist her clients to master wellness and optimal health through cognitive and behavioural change.

From 1990 to 2010, Minda pursued a successful career with a range of global technology companies. One of these included her role as state manager (Queensland and Northern Territory, Australia) for Computer Associates, where she was nominated in 2005 for the Optus Challenger Spirit Award, Industry Achievement for Women in Technology.

After holding a number of strategic sales and senior management positions in both Australia and the United Kingdom, Minda decided to concentrate on her passion for fitness and wellbeing by establishing Figure 8 Wellness in 2010. She is now focused exclusively on using her innate coaching, management and goal-setting skills to help women from all walks of life to achieve balance, empowerment and extraordinary wellness. As a wellness coach, she focuses on mental and physical behaviours relating to nutrition, exercise, weight control, stress management and Wheel of Life balance.

Minda has always maintained a steady commitment to eating well and exercising regularly, while balancing career and family life. After two previous attempts at competing, she achieved third place as Novice Figure Competitor at the International Natural Bodybuilding Association (INBA) QLD Titles in October 2005 – a great result as it was exactly seven months after giving birth to her second child. Four competitions and two years later, Minda finally placed second as an Open Figure competitor at the World Natural Bodybuilding Federation (WNBF) Asia–Pacific Championships.

Minda is also a happy and busy working mum of two beautiful girls (Jazmin, 9 and Samara, 6) and wife to her 'adorable' husband, best friend and life partner, Phil. Her most recent ventures into writing include the eBook *8 Skips to Extraordinary Wellness,* the article series *Extraordinary Wellness for Working Mums* based on Wheel of Life balance, the blog *For Women Seeking Wellness,* and her soon-to-be-published first book *I am woman – the art of being you.*

You Are Brilliant, Gorgeous, Talented and Fabulous – Inside and Out!

MINDA LENNON

Many of us live out our lives saying we'll take a step forward when we're not so scared and have more confidence, more choices, more energy, more time or more money. Then we find we never take the step because the fear doesn't fade, our confidence never goes up – it even goes down – the choices don't present themselves, our energy depletes even further, time slips away and the money never comes.

These incessant fears and excuses keep us from skipping, jumping in puddles, stubbing our toes … LIVING! Every time we put 'avoiding fear' ahead of our true desires, we're preventing ourselves from truly appreciating and loving our lives, and we fail to give ourselves the chance to live the life of our dreams!

I know because this was ME. I had an overworked husband working remotely, two young children craving my attention, my own full-time corporate career and a tendency to take on more and more. I was always putting others first while feeling guilty about not getting everything done. I spent my days feeling like I was letting myself down because I wasn't following my heart and doing all the things I said I would do by this stage in my life. The chatter of the little 'mini-me' voices in my head constantly reinforced my self-limiting beliefs about my perceived lack of success in all areas – including my body not being at its best. I hated being apart from my loved ones and I had an overwhelming feeling that my life was going by too fast. I'd lost control.

All the while I was craving and wishing I had more time and money to spend on the things I really value and love: the people in my life (my husband, my beautiful daughters, my family, my girlfriends); my freedom; my health and fitness; my happiness; travelling; helping others; good food and a great bottle of wine; music; laughter; fun; walking on the beach; downtime; silence; sleep. I had an authentic need to be valued and feel good enough.

What could I do to stop myself from falling apart? I certainly didn't want to get through another year or more thinking *If only* ... I knew I could either sink or swim because I have been there before and done them both while trying to 'do it all'. I definitely did not want to sink because when I sink – buckling under the pressure of feeling overworked, overwhelmed and lacking motivation – I sink DEEP. As time moves on, I then start to feel like I'm in a rut, unclear about what to do. So, I end up doing nothing because the risk in taking action appears too great. At this point, I usually stop playing the 'game of life' because it's not fun anymore and I begin to let my fears hold me back.

But this time I decided to FLY! Looking back, really, it was easy. Or should I say it was easy once I knew where I wanted to go. In fact, for me it was more about realising what I didn't want and recognising that my life was so out of balance that I was heading for a personal breakdown; so I knew that the only way forward was to act fast and act big. Wishing my life was easier was a waste of time; I had to believe I could be better!

By taking a step back, assessing what was missing in my life and allowing myself the space and time to dream without fear, I began to see the pathway to success. Within a matter of weeks, through consistent focus, goal setting and baby steps, I gradually became the person I needed to be and started doing the things I needed to do to positively influence my life's outcomes. My priorities were very clear, so I changed careers and decided to put myself, my health and my family first.

You see, *courage/confidence is not the absence of fear but the willingness to take action despite it.* In fact you can't learn courage unless you take action. This is the ultimate paradox. I needed to do the thing that scared me the most to make me realise and trust I had the courage and resources within me to achieve great things. And this is the same for you.

Now, I perceive success to be everywhere, especially in those ecstatic moments of everyday life that quite simply take my breath away. I see it in my daughters' smiles when they come down the stairs in the morning and see me waiting to make them breakfast. I feel it in my husband's warm embrace when he returns home on a Thursday night from his weekly commute to Sydney. I hear it in my client's voice when I finish a coaching session – such empowerment, such commitment, such strength. I taste it at the dinner table over candlelight with my close family and friends. I smell it in the air with the scent of Star Jasmine wafting past the clothesline as I hang out the washing. I touch it when I feel the salt air on my face blowing off the ocean as I stand on the deck of my beautiful home on the headland at Moffat Beach.

You can do this, too! By focusing on what you value, finding out what you are passionate about, expecting the best, eliminating self-limiting beliefs and negativity, and letting go of your fears and frustrations *you can live a life of purpose with an abundance of energy, self-respect, self-love, self-truth, self-forgiveness and self-esteem.*

Let me just remind you that your past and future exists in the endless moments of 'now'. Your memories determine who you are now and your self-esteem is shaped by what you are willing to be in the future.

- *Are you ready to embrace vulnerability, stop playing safe and act even when you feel fear?*
- *Are you ready to be the best you can be, in all ways, for always?*
- *Are you ready to draw a line in the sand and start with the present to influence your future?*

If you answered 'yes' to any of the above, then it's time to *take action, massive action – right now.* You deserve it. Be prepared to invest in yourself, in any way necessary. Attempt great things for you and expect great things from you. From my own experience, I can reassure you that if you are committed to start living a life with a sense of purpose, you will be empowered to make your life one of significance, joy and extraordinary wellness. It all starts with choosing new beliefs.

Minda and her beautiful daughters

Extraordinary Wellness is Your Choice

I'd like to help you get started by encouraging you to think about what new beliefs you will choose to play by. Here are a few suggestions:

- *As a mother, daughter, sister, lover, wife, manager, employee and friend I have nothing to prove and nothing to defend.*
- *The greatest gift I can give myself is self-respect — I choose to be and remain loyal to myself.*
- *The greatest gift I can give my children is to lead a life by example — I choose to support myself daily on my path to wellness and give myself freedom to live every day with energy, vitality and unconditional love.*

Whatever new beliefs you choose, just start LIVING. Choose TODAY to be a greater version of YOU and LIVE a life of Energy, Vitality and Purpose!

'The strongest principle of growth lies in human choice.' ~ *George Eliot*

My approach to wellness is a holistic one where one places equal importance and relevance on the health, energy and vitality of both the mind and the body. Wellness can be defined as the optimal balance of body, mind and spirit, integrated and dynamic, all working toward maximising your potential dependence on self-responsibility. It is obtained through the process of adopting patterns of behaviour that exemplify heightened or conscious awareness to provide you with positive health and an optimal quality of life.

So, how does one develop heightened awareness? Well, it starts with *mindset* – a set of assumptions, methods or notations held by one or a group of people which is so established that it creates a powerful incentive to continue to adopt or accept prior behaviours or choices[2], irrespective of whether they are positive or negative. It is simply your mental framework – your own set of attitudes, expectations and prejudices.

Extraordinary can be defined as going beyond what is usual, regular or customary ... to be exceptional! Therefore, it stands to reason that if you create a mindset for extraordinary wellness then you must adopt patterns of behaviour that exemplify heightened awareness. With conscious awareness you have the ability to change your values, beliefs, reality and reactions to directly and positively influence your desired outcomes.

Just *choosing* to make wellness a priority in your life will empower you to make a start towards a healthier you. Then by taking consistent action one step at a time, you will maximise your potential for optimal balance of physical and mental health.

Extraordinary wellness is a choice and you have all the resources needed for extraordinary wellness within you right now – even if you are not focused on them YET!

The Mind/Body Connection

Have you ever heard the saying 'What you focus on is what you get?' The body you have right now is the body you believe you deserve and has taken years and years of dedication and mental focus to create.

Mental wellness or illness creates a physical outcome EVERY time, without fail. The mind and body are part of an interactive system. Anything that happens in one part of the system affects all parts of the system.

2 Wikipedia http://en.wikipedia.org/wiki/Mindset

We cannot, for example, have a thought without having a physical response to that thought as all thought and information from the brain are communicated to the body through a multitude of neurotransmitters. Your body is always telling you what is happening and your mind only knows how to communicate symbolically through your body. So, what I'm trying to stress here is the power of your own mind regarding your health.

What's more, your unconscious mind has a blueprint of perfect health. It has all the answers and knows how to heal. You just have to hear it and trust it. Are you really listening? For instance, digestive and stomach issues are directly linked to your feelings of power or powerlessness. Have you lost the ability to say no? If so, you have lost or given your power away, and this could be causing your digestive and stomach issues. The neurons in your stomach lining are bigger than the neurons in your brain and your stomach renews itself every five days. Your stomach lining will replace an ulcer if your mind has not released the emotional connection creating this physical reaction. Interesting, isn't it?

> *'The more severe the pain or illness,*
> *the more severe will be the necessary changes.*
>
> *These may involve breaking old habits,*
> *or acquiring some new and better ones.'*
>
> ~ *Peter McWilliams*

Therefore, the health of your mind plays an enormous role in your overall physical health and wellbeing. By focusing on your mental wellbeing, you can positively influence your physical state. You can improve your metabolic and immune system responses, reduce or eliminate chronic pain and inflammation (which lessens the need for drug intervention), and improve muscular health, mobility and recovery. The number of 'feel good' hormones in your brain can be dramatically increased; thus promoting a positive and sustainable cycle of mental wellness.

Imagine the positive impact mental wellness can have on chronic diseases such as depression, obesity, diabetes, arthritis, heart disease and cancer. In fact, many new thought healers believe that if a person is one hundred per cent focused on happy thoughts, without any resistance, one hundred per cent of the time, any dis-ease in the body will disappear.

So, my goal in this chapter is to provide you with the knowledge and tools for living a life of EXTRAORDINARY WELLNESS, a wellness within the mind and the body. There are three important keys to achieving this:

- **MINDSET:** First you must guide, expand and reframe your unconscious and conscious minds to where you need them to be to support your extraordinary wellness journey. You then need to nourish, train and strengthen your body – your temple. Having the right mindset is crucial. Without it, you won't be able to succeed in following the next two keys.

- **CONSCIOUS EATING:** If you have access to healthy food and you're responsible for what you eat, you have the power to choose good nutrition and give your body the best possible defence against illness.

- **DAILY MOVEMENT:** Daily movement is critical for us to develop strength and stability and to maintain minimal levels of health and fitness. We need to maintain a balance in our energies, between our energy input and output. An imbalance can result in weight gain or weight loss. Daily movement will not just benefit our physical state but emotional and mental as well.

First Key: An Empowering Mindset

'Most folks are about as happy as they make up their minds to be.'
~ Abraham Lincoln

Early on in my career as a personal trainer, I noticed that my clients often failed to maintain a constant focus when not in personal training. I realised I needed to find a way to influence their thinking so they could empower, support and nurture themselves when I was not with them, which was usually for around 166 hours out of 168 hours in a week.

You see it does not matter what you do in your one-on-one personal training sessions. In fact it is often a waste of money, time and effort (sweat!) if your mindset, self-talk and beliefs are sabotaging your physical efforts. And that's what I found happening consistently with my clients.

Something about their self-talk and self-belief was undermining their efforts to succeed in their wellness.

I started to ask myself, 'What impact can I have with my clients when they are not with me? How can I empower them to believe they ARE more, can DO more, BE more and HAVE more?'

I then began asking each of my clients more empowering questions such as those below.

Please take a moment now to answer these questions for yourself:

- *How do you want to feel every day?*
- *What are you trying to achieve?*
- *What is your motivation?*
- *What are you willing to change to achieve this?*
- *What are you not willing to change?*
- *If you achieved it, what would be different?*
- *What would be the best thing that could happen?*
- *What would be the worst thing that could happen?*
- *If you failed to achieve it, what consequences would that bring?*

It's always the goal, the irresistible and compelling outcome that drives the action and the commitment! It's about deciding what you value and what your standard of excellence is. It's about being uncompromising in your adherence to those principles in every facet of your life. It's about setting the bar for yourself and others. It's about being a Winner in your own game of life! To do that, you need a mindset. And that's what I was setting up in my clients. I was challenging their existing mindset and encouraging them to adopt a new one if the old one wasn't working!

As mentioned earlier, the first key, mindset, refers to your mental framework. Adopting an empowering mindset is one of the greatest life strategies there is. By using powerful positive thinking techniques, positive affirmations and visualisations, you can attain whatever it is in life you desire. In the business world, professionals practise these techniques to influence others, expand their personal power or gain a competitive advantage.

On a more personal level, an empowering mindset will improve your health, energy and vitality — re-igniting your passion and purpose for life. The transformation really is that powerful!

If you DO choose an empowering mindset you WILL:

- *improve your wellness and set better goals, motivating you in a healthy way*
- *achieve great awareness, balance and success in your personal and professional life*
- *expand your comfort zone and transform problems into possibilities*
- *learn to embrace abundance in your career and finances*
- *achieve sustainable happiness with reduced stress and no more excuses*
- *become an expert communicator, benefiting every relationship in your life*
- *attract others through genuine rapport and influence*
- *improve your chances of living a life of purpose*

> *'It's choice - not chance — that determines your destiny.'*
> *~ Jean Nidetch*

Ultimately, you will start living 'at cause', believing you are one hundred per cent responsible for what happens in your life. Living at cause means owning your moods, your emotions and your responses and realising that there is a difference between reacting and responding. Conversely, living 'at effect' means reacting to the emotions and desires of others. Reacting comes from fear, whereas responding comes through learning, considering and then responding. It is about being on fire, striving for excellence, conscious awareness and results. And every result will be yours to own.

To you, more choices will equal more empowerment. With this awareness, you will have the ability to move forward without fear of failure because you understand failure is only feedback, and you will just try something different to get a different result. You will let go of your excuses, blame or denial. You will realise that by taking responsibility for your results and non-results you are giving yourself a far greater opportunity to change your results.

At the moment you may not be living at cause, but you do have all you need within you to experience the reality you want. Right now, you can change how you react to your experiences and start living the life you desire. You need to focus on what you want, set big goals and then create the mindset that will support you to move towards them, step by step. Your mind is a goal-setting machine and will do whatever is necessary to lead and inspire you to greatness, if you let it.

We have been raised in a culture to be slaves.
Why can't we condition ourselves to live as QUEENS?

You can choose, instantly, to turn things around through your internal resourcefulness rather than external resources. You just need to start with making a commitment and taking ownership. I encourage you to make that commitment immediately. Choose to live at cause and take ownership for your emotions, experiences and your outcomes.

You can choose right now to adopt a mindset that will transform your life for extraordinary wellness, empower you to live as a queen and inspire your kingdom!

So for the rest of this chapter, I encourage you to adopt the mindset of an Olympic athlete and let's see how close you get towards achieving GOLD!

You may be striving for a variety of outcomes in your health, fitness and overall wellness. It may be to lose weight or improve fitness, functionality or performance. It may be to improve your body shape or self-image. It may also be to reduce pain or prevent further illness. Whatever it is, just remember there is no right way to train. It is whatever works for you and your unique needs – and it all starts with mindset!

Go back over this chapter again and again and again – whenever you feel the need to replenish, refresh and reinvigorate your motivation. Your body deserves your unconditional, tireless commitment to excellence. You only get one shot at life, so make sure your temple is at its absolute best!

Now, let's move onto the second key to achieving extraordinary wellness: conscious eating.

Second Key: Conscious Eating

'We are indeed much more than what we eat, but what we eat can nevertheless help us to be much more than what we are.'

~ Adelle Davis

Conscious eating is fundamental to a healthy life. When you are consciously aware of what you are eating, you can consciously choose to change it. There are so many confusing messages, marketing hype and fad diets, and depriving yourself is not the answer. Life is about pleasure and, believe me, there is nothing pleasurable about dieting! Get off the diet treadmill and make a promise to yourself right now to stop harming your body with fad diets. Instead, become consciously aware of the food you are choosing to eat.

The best way to gain awareness about the type of food you are consuming on a daily basis is by keeping a nutritional journal or food diary. This will encourage you to develop a healthy relationship with the food you eat. So start keeping a journal. By recording every bite you eat, you will get an exact overview of what types of foods you consume on a daily basis. The longer you catalogue your food consumption, the more you will see patterns emerge. Conscious awareness of what you are eating, how much and when, then identifying the triggers motivating you to eat, are the first steps in changing unhealthy eating habits.

For example, if you notice that you snack on unhealthy food every day around 3 pm, you may choose to defeat that urge by distracting yourself with an outdoor activity like a long walk, or replacing your unhealthy snack with a serving of fruit, vegetables or nuts and seeds.

Okay, let's go back to basics now and see what we do actually need to consume.

For survival, the human body needs:

- *Nutrients*
- *Oxygen*
- *Water*
- *Stable body temperature*
- *Appropriate atmospheric pressure*

At this point, I will assume that the atmospheric pressure where you live is of no consequence and you have abundant oxygen, water and a stable body temperature. But what about nutrition? Many chronic diseases are linked to poor nutrition. Heart disease, hypertension, cancer, gallstones, diabetes, osteoporosis, arthritis, Alzheimer's, depression, stroke and obesity are all connected to what you put in your mouth.

If you have access to healthy food and you are responsible for what you eat, you have the power to choose good nutrition. The message is simple: eat to nourish your body, NOT to lose weight, and give your body the best possible defence against illness!

Choosing healthy food for good nutrition is actually very simple and easy. Just fill your grocery trolley primarily with foods that don't have labels. You know, the ones that are real, whole, unprocessed and only one step removed from their original source, for example, the apple tree. Basically, eat real food your great-grandmother would recognise – food fit for a queen!

And drink more water, please – filtered is best. Chronic dehydration places severe stress on the body and is now being implicated in an increasing number of chronic diseases. Most people do not drink enough to replenish their body each day. The easiest way to track and increase your daily water intake is to *keep a record* – aim for *a glass of water upon rising* to rehydrate from the night then *a glass each hour until bed,* marking down in your food diary the number of glasses you have had.

Eat to nourish your body, NOT to lose weight, and give your body the best possible defence against illness!

Now, I do understand how it feels at the end of a busy day to be so depleted of energy and time that you reach for the take-away menus, frozen dinners – anything fast. This is what I call slave food. It is fast, processed, pre-packaged, full of chemicals and preservatives, and energy dense (high in calories). But it is nutritionally empty and unsustainable – unsustainable for your health, your wellness and your life in general. I still have those moments when convenience is king; it's just now I consciously choose not to let them become a consistent habit. I enjoy the treat, appreciate the release of pressure and make sure it's nutritious, healthy and of course yummy!

When designing your daily menu, use the **80/20 rule** – eighty per cent real foods (real, fresh, whole, nutrient-rich food with high water content that is also usually low in calories and is enjoyed slowly) and twenty per cent processed foods. Your body will love you for it, I promise! It is so easy, fast and convenient to grab an apple, a carrot or a handful of nuts.

Third Key: Daily Movement and Energy Balance

Daily movement is critical for us to develop strength and stability and to maintain minimal levels of health and fitness. Whether you are underweight, normal weight or overweight, all comes down to the balance between the energy we expend (Energy Output) through movement and the energy we take in (Energy Input) via foods. Our dietary practices will affect this energy balance, as will the amount of exercise we perform and the amount of stress we are under.

Our bodies have an unlimited ability to store fat and will store carbohydrates as fat if they are unused as an energy source. We are, however, unable to store protein, which is why some fad diets promote a high protein intake. Did you know that your body will always burn alcohol before other food sources? Hence, eliminating alcohol from your diet can dramatically improve your chances of weight loss, especially if you replace it with water!

Your body weight is usually relatively stable if the Energy Input (EI) and Energy Output (EO) remain about equal; you are burning off what you take in. Energy Input includes all food and alcohol and Energy Output includes all exercise and physical activity.

If Energy Input is greater than the Energy Output it will result in a positive energy balance, thus producing weight gain.

Weight loss will occur if the Energy Input (EI) is less than the Energy Output (EO).

It's all in the balance between what you put in and what you put out!

Your hormones and the health of your thyroid also affect how your body can work at its optimum and to some extent can dictate your metabolic rate and body weight stability. Unfortunately, both can be negatively impacted by stress. Prolonged stress, which results in sustained, high levels of the stress hormone cortisol, can cause the metabolic rate to slow down to conserve energy. This encourages the body to store fat and can often impair mental processes. Hence, the importance of reducing stress where possible!

Exercise is an important constituent in controlling and reducing the impact of stress on your body. In fact, post-exercise the stress hormone reduces dramatically.

> *'Movement is a medicine for creating change in a person's*
> *physical, emotional and mental states.'*
> ~ *Carol Welch*

Daily movement is critical for us to develop strength and stability and to maintain minimal levels of health and fitness. We all have our own motivations for improved health and fitness. For people suffering from chronic disease, degeneration, depression and pain, it may be the desire to move and feel better. For the moderately active person, it may be the desire for more energy and vitality and an increased ability to perform everyday tasks with limited pain or discomfort.

Whatever your motivation, just start moving and focus on your goal of getting healthier when exercising rather than weight loss! It doesn't need to be in a gym; it doesn't need to be at a certain time of day; AND it doesn't have to be for a certain length of time in one session. The optimum I recommend is 45–60 minutes each day of a combination of strength and aerobic exercise. Of course, be realistic as to where you are now in your fitness level and seek guidance from a trainer as to what's an appropriate program for your current state of fitness. Step by step you'll get there! Each tiny achievement will empower you.

I know what it's like to feel as if you are just juggling too many balls and can't (or won't) take the time you need to exercise or watch what you're eating – particularly after having a baby.

The wise women who bestow on us the information that 'Having a baby changes everything' always have this sort of mysterious knowing (or was that ominous?) smile. But until I had my first child (I have two beautiful girls), the 'everything' just did not sink in. You see, I had a plan ...

I had everything from maternity leave, to juggling the household chores, to who would care for the kids when I returned to work well mapped out. After all, I was an accomplished businesswoman who kept her life, body (and hair) in as top form as her career. Yet when it came to knowing just how much my life would change after childbirth ... I was absolutely clueless!

There is just no way to fully appreciate the absolute joy of new motherhood along with the overwhelming feeling of seeing your life spin out of control – and your body along with it. Perhaps you can relate? Before children, there generally is time to focus on your diet, exercise and health. Then during pregnancy we start eating for two and any exercise – other than those breathing exercises in preparation for labour – is the last thing on our minds.

After baby arrives, where on earth do you find the time, energy and motivation to plan healthy meals or hit the gym when you are already juggling parenthood, being a wife, working and the newly found dilemma of taking a daily shower, let alone washing your hair?

If you are a busy working mum who is time- and energy-poor and feeling that somewhere along the way you have lost control; if you are interested in not only losing weight but in enjoying optimal health, fitness, energy and vitality; believe me – you CAN succeed! You just need *a plan* that works for you then commit to action. That is what I did.

I sat down and made a realistic schedule and stuck to it. I made sure I did my cardio every morning after my baby's first feed (usually around 5:00 am) and before my toddler got up. Then I fitted in my strength

> *There is just no way to fully appreciate the absolute joy of new motherhood along with the overwhelming feeling of seeing your life spin out of control – and your body along with it.*

training throughout the day in snippets. It was not perfect and every day was different, but it worked for me.

My third attempt at a figure competition (body sculpting rather than body building) was seven months after the birth of my second daughter AND I managed to take out third place! Trust me when I say I was time-poor with a new baby and a three-year-old toddler. But I had a plan, I was committed and I trained at home with a treadmill, hand weights and a fit ball.

'Always bear in mind that your own resolution to succeed is more important than any one thing.'
~ *Abraham Lincoln*

Action Tools for Extraordinary Wellness

We have now overviewed what I consider to be the three main keys to extraordinary wellness: an empowering mindset; a conscious, nutritional plan; plus a consistent, ongoing commitment to moving every day. It is now time to bring this all together with a simple tool to support you on your path to wellness, giving you freedom to live every day with energy and vitality.

Affirmations, the words you choose to speak to yourself and others, can be very powerful. You may want to write affirmations about your abundant energy, vitality and health then stick them up on your mirror or in your calendar, wherever you will see them, and then say them several times a day. Post up pictures of your pre-pregnancy, younger, fitter self or of role models, too. You can also create this using other methods such as a *vision board.*

This helps to convince your conscious mind that health and fitness is on its way and soon you will have the body you desire. Your unconscious mind already knows this to be true and what you choose to focus on becomes your reality! So get focused!

'Life's about skipping with energy, vitality and purpose, NOT losing weight!'
~ *Minda Lennon*

The final step is all about creating a plan using your empowering mindset and taking action. By agreeing and committing to clearly defined goals, actions and timeframes, you are mentally preparing yourself to improve your health and live the life you deserve. Without a clear plan I would never have shed my post-baby weight or gone on to compete in body sculpting competitions, let alone win third place. Formulating a plan and setting goals allows you to create a roadmap for life, a clear vision for how you are going to get to wherever it is you want to go. I encourage you to use something, anything, everything! Whatever you need to do is right for you because self-improvement, continual learning and hard work make the recipe for success.

To achieve extraordinary growth, the type of growth that taps into your true life purpose and brings you great joy and happiness, putting you in touch with your own magnificence, requires continual commitment and constant action that will challenge and stretch you greater than ever before. I know you can do it! Choose TODAY to be a greater version of YOU!

Suggestions for You to Live With Extraordinary Wellness

 Choose to have an empowering mindset

Self-improvement: Just as I have, you can CHOOSE TODAY to be a greater version of you! Adopt an empowering mindset to support your extraordinary wellness journey. You already have all the resources within you and know how to access them to bring about change and success.

 Continually learn

Be prepared to invest in yourself in any way necessary! Start by identifying what specific resources you need in order to achieve your extraordinary wellness goals. Is everything you need readily available or do you need to take action to gain access to them? Is this something you can do by yourself or do you need outside help, such as a wellness coach, life coach or personal trainer, medical intervention, dietary advice, gym membership or training equipment?

 Take action – MASSIVE ACTION – right now!

Make a list of all of the resources you need then work out if they are readily available or whether you need to take action to gain access to them as above. Remember, the time you spend on yourself represents the value you place on yourself. You are worthy of every second, minute, hour, day, week, month and year you wish to dedicate to your personal development and growth.

GET YOUR EXTRAORDINARY
FREE GIFT BONUS

Minda Lennon is kindly offering a **FREE BONUS GIFT** to all readers of this book.

Extraordinary Wellness for Working Mums

An 8-article Series for achieving Wheel of Life balance.

Simply visit the web page below and follow the directions to directly download *Extraordinary Wellness for Working Mums*.

www.figure8wellness.com.au/content/free_stuff/register

'Only when we respect, honour, love, trust and appreciate ourselves are we truly able to do the same for others and thus sustain enduring, loving relationships.'

Ghania Dib BCom LLB (Hons)

Ghania Dib has had a lifelong fascination with what constitutes loving, fulfilling, lifelong relationships. She believes that the relationships we harbour and nurture define our life experiences and are at the core of what constitutes an extraordinary life.

As both a practising lawyer in Sydney, Australia, with an interest in Family Law, and a freelance journalist in the area of family relations and parenting, Ghania saw far too often the personal devastation that accompanied relationship and matrimonial breakdown. It was after the breakdown of her own marriage that she turned a fascination into a journey of self-awareness and subsequently a profession.

Ghania is now a Certified Life and Performance Coach, NLP Practitioner, Practitioner of Matrix Therapy, Accredited Consultant & Trainer of Extended DISC, Human Behaviour Specialist, Certified Mediator and Motivational Speaker. She has also trained with Dr Bradley Nelson in the 'Emotion Code' and believes that we all possess the ability to be the authors of our own destiny.

She is passionate about assisting and empowering others, as authors of their own destiny, to create and sustain loving, fulfilling relationships with themselves and others. To this end she has founded Philosophy - Live, Love & Thrive, a personal and relationship coaching practice which aims to educate and empower others in their journey towards their own unique definition of personal fulfillment. Drawing on her years in the corporate sector, Ghania also founded Ghania Dib & Associates, an Australian-based consultancy firm specialising in the provision of corporate and executive coaching.

According to Ghania, she is first and foremost a mother, a daughter, a sister and a friend who is passionate about making the most of her life experiences. She credits her mother for the person that she is today and the memory of her mother's words that she can achieve anything and everything if she has the dedication, passion and persistence to do so, have guided her through her toughest challenges.

Ghania has always loved writing and is passionate about using the written word to touch the hearts and lives of others. She is currently co-authoring a book on the often overlooked topic of *Motherloss*, to be published mid-2012.

Live, Love and Thrive

GHANIA DIB

Have you ever stopped to reflect on what constitutes an extraordinary life?

Too often in life, we stumble ahead from day to day, doing the same old routine, repeating the same old behaviours and ridiculously expecting better results. We dream of a life filled with passion, excitement, spontaneity and purpose. Yet most of us are too afraid to step outside the boundaries of our existence, boundaries which are often self-imposed. It's no secret that we humans are creatures of habit. We have an infinite capacity to dream about living a life with purpose yet few of us really know what that means, and the pressures of modern life often leave us with little time or energy to reflect on this very issue.

I have always loved inspiration in its many forms, be it books, quotes, music, poetry or Oprah. But the truth is it's easy to be inspired and happy and dream of a better future when life is good. Unfortunately, it's not so easy to be inspired when life knocks you down and kicks you up the butt. After all, it takes just one defining moment, one life-changing event, to knock you off your feet.

What happens, however, when you're dealt a number of defining moments in a matter of a few short years? When you lose your mother suddenly and way too prematurely? When you lose a baby to miscarriage, your husband pretends you were never pregnant in the first place and you feel you have no one to turn to for support? When you suffer from depression, spending weeks on end crying because the thought of 'Is this is as good as it gets?' is slowly killing you on the inside? When your best friend and husband repeatedly breaks your heart into a million-and-one pieces and you're left sobbing on the ground wondering where it all went wrong? When you're cruising down the road one morning and you're suddenly involved in a head-on collision that leaves you slipping in and out of consciousness as you silently pray to God to allow you to live and to return home to your three young children?

How, when faced with a series of defining moments, do you find the courage and the strength to pick yourself up and keep on moving ahead, one small step after the other, toward a life lived more consciously and filled with purpose?

I was lucky enough to not only have survived the above events, but for such events to have (in time) become the catalyst of a journey of self-awareness and growth that culminated in me finally living a life filled (for the most part) with purpose, variety and passion.

Relationships: At the Core of an Extraordinary Life

When it comes to death and the loss of loved ones, there really is little we can do to control the situation. One of the facts of life is that all that is born must one day cease to be. The best we can do when we lose a loved one is to give ourselves the permission to grieve, to seek support and to hold on to the belief that one day we will once again find joy in daily life.

In comparison, the death of a relationship is an experience that is within our sphere of influence. Most often relationships break down because there is a disconnection on some level, a presence of undesirable behaviours or an absence of desirable behaviours. When the behaviours in question are our own, they are within our direct sphere of influence. We are still in a position to exert some level of influence when the behaviour in question does not belong to us because although we may not be able to control the behaviours of our loved ones, we certainly have the power to control how we respond to such behaviour. As such, it is my contention that we are accountable for the outcome of our relationships, whatever that outcome may be.

If you were to take a minute and reflect on what is truly important in your life, what would your answer be? Close your eyes for a minute and ask yourself that very question, and then listen to the answer that comes deep from within your unconscious mind.

For me, it's my relationship with my-self and others and my purpose in life, which derives from such relations. Without my internal and external connections, I am certain that my life would be far from extraordinary and would feel empty and void of any real joy. Money and power may give us a temporary thrill ... but deep, enduring happiness? That comes from feeling connected and loved and from living a life filled with purpose.

Put simply, *relationships are at the heart of an extraordinary life.*

As you would have gathered, I use the term 'relationship' to refer to our intimate relationship with our significant other, our relationships with our friends and family, and our relationship with our-selves. Relationship with self is a dynamic that is far too often overlooked in favour of our external relationships, and yet it is the one relationship that dictates the outcome of almost every other relationship in our lives.

Money and power may give us a temporary thrill ... but deep, enduring happiness? That comes from feeling connected and loved and from living a life filled with purpose.

I discovered the hard way that my external world was a reflection of my internal world and my relationship with my-self. As long as there was a state of internal chaos created by a failure on my part to care for and love my-self, there would be mistrust of others and external chaos. My relationship with my-self dictated the outcome of one of the most important relationships in my life – my relationship with my then-husband. Unsurprisingly, it was not the outcome I had hoped for.

Although many of us believe that happy, fulfilling relationships are the core of an extraordinary life, no one consciously teaches us how to live a life filled with purpose and passion, or how to create and develop deep, fulfilling connections with ourselves and others. As children, we observe our parents. Their behaviours and habits, regardless of whether or not they serve us, become embedded deep within our unconscious mind. As adults, we spend many years wishing for a better life, yet often find ourselves inadvertently returning to the very behaviours that hold us back. And not surprisingly, those behaviours are almost always a result of the beliefs and expectations we adopted as children.

I was blessed to have had one of the most amazing mothers to have walked the earth. She was one of the most loving, self-sacrificing people I have ever met. She was, quite simply, a martyr, who would put her own life on the line for the safety, security and happiness of her children.

As a result of my observations of the way my mother lived her life, and my consequent belief that self-sacrifice was a virtue, I unconsciously decided when I got married that my husband and children would come first.

As a result of my observations of the way my mother lived her life, and my consequent belief that self-sacrifice was a virtue, I unconsciously decided when I got married that my husband and children would come first. I believed with all my heart that simply loving my partner and being a good mother and wife would be enough to sustain my marriage and give me a life filled with purpose and meaning.

I had, however, a long-held, deep hidden desire to be somebody of consequence, a desire which as an adult I guiltily pushed away because I was afraid that by acknowledging my own desires I would jeopardise the wellbeing of my family. I couldn't have been farther from the truth.

By becoming the same self-sacrificing woman that I believed my mother was, I attributed little significance to my own wellbeing. I defined my happiness by the state of my marriage. When my marriage was proceeding along nicely, I was happy; when it wasn't, I was miserable.

I expected my husband to complete me, and without so much as telling him so I held him accountable for my happiness. I had, to use the words of Elizabeth Gilbert, expected my husband to be my best friend, my most intimate confidant, my emotional advisor, my intellectual equal and my comfort in times of sorrow.[3] When he failed to live up to such an onerous expectation, I became disappointed and frustrated. And when he hurt me in a way I had never conceived possible, I was left heartbroken and disillusioned, wondering where I had gone wrong.

His behaviour became a reflection of my own self-worth, rather than a reflection of his own internal demons. I held myself accountable for the choices he made in his life and consequently engaged in a never ending barrage of self-criticism ranging from 'I'm not good enough' to 'I'm not beautiful enough' to 'Maybe, I'm just not lovable'.

In an attempt to control the situation, I began to anticipate his future behaviour. Not surprisingly, my expectations often became my reality. Other times, I abandoned control in favour of being reactionary and failed to take ownership of my ability to reflect and respond from a space of self-awareness. Accordingly, I had little understanding of how my own behaviour had contributed to the situation I had (much to own dismay) found myself in.

My confidence suffered terribly and I had no concept of self-love. To say that I felt depressed, depleted and hopeless would be an understatement. I had no idea how to make things better and yet I stubbornly held on to the belief that I could somehow singlehandedly prevent my marriage from becoming another statistic.

To make matters worse, I had early on in my marriage isolated myself and was unable to derive emotional support and nourishment from friends and family. I endured some of the most challenging moments in my life on my own. I had single-handedly dug myself into a hole and needed a ladder to climb back out. I had no idea, however, where that ladder would come from or how long it would be before I could climb back up.

The decision to leave my husband was one of the most difficult decisions I have ever made. If you have ever had to walk away from

---

[3] Elizabeth Gilbert; *Committed – A sceptic makes peace with marriage*; P 32.

someone you love, you would have a sense of what I mean. He once said that it would take the breakdown of our marriage for me to abandon mistrust and find happiness and inner peace.

Unfortunately, he was right.

It wasn't the act of leaving him that gave me back my inner peace, happiness and trust. It was, however, the beginning of a journey that finally led me towards living an extraordinary life filled with a deep sense of internal peace, happiness, passion, excitement and purpose. A life where self-love takes centre stage and becomes the source from which I am able to reflect love externally towards my children, family, friends and humanity in general.

It was the beginning of a journey that finally led me towards living an extraordinary life filled with a deep sense of internal peace, happiness, passion, excitement and purpose.

As a result of the failure of my marriage, I became intrigued by what it was that enabled a marriage to sustain and survive the pressures of modern life and the inherent differences between men and women. What is it that, in the midst of all the gloomy statistics about marriage and divorce, allowed two people to spend their lives together in happy matrimony? Surely there was some secret that I had not yet uncovered.

I commenced my search for answers on Tuesday. Every Tuesday to be precise. While the writer Mitch Albom had **Tuesdays with Morrie,** I was fortunate enough to have Tuesdays with Larry, a seventy-something-year-old therapist and life coach who I came to love and respect over my eighteen-month journey with him. I learnt much about my-self and about marriage and relationships during our time together. I began to understand the complexities of the human psyche entwined with our deep desires to be loved and to belong. And for the first time in my life, I began to understand my-self.

Upon embracing self-love and awareness, and finally feeling like I was a complete woman devoid of any lack, I became curious about the interplay between men and women, and in particular how their own unique energies played out in intimate relationships. I read every book I could find on the topic of relationships and men. I experimented with the concepts I came across and challenged my old beliefs and ways of thinking.

I reflected in solitude on the relationship between a happy, fulfilled woman and a happy, fulfilling marriage. I became curious about learning about and from happily married couples, where both husband and wife lived a life filled with passion, excitement and purpose.

My readings and reflections certainly assisted my personal growth and provided me with some of the answers I had sought. However, the secrets to living an extraordinary life filled with passion and purpose, regardless of whether or not one is in a marriage or intimate relationship, were not revealed to me until my journey led me to an in-depth study of human behaviour and the interplay between feminine and masculine energies.

The Power of Self-Love

'I celebrate my-self, and sing my-self' ~ *Walt Whitman*

Many of us women were raised by mothers who were skilled at serving everyone else's needs before their own. As a result, most of us have been conditioned to equate being a woman with being selfless. We shy away from looking after our own desires, feel guilty about saying no and about respecting our boundaries, and those of us who are married toss and turn in our beds wondering if we are good enough mothers and wives.

I remember only too clearly spending every minute of my time either working from my home office or serving my family's interests. There was never any time-out allocated in my day for me to just be. I became neurotic about doing everything after my mother passed away. I oddly believed that I was honouring her memory by emulating her self-sacrifice. I now know that had she been around to see the way I had self-sacrificed myself and my time, she would have sat

I had to learn the hard way that although being a mum and a wife was an important part of my life, it was not all of who I was.

me down and given me a stern talk about the importance of self-love.

For far too long, I had pushed the parts of me that I deemed self-centred away. Not surprisingly, I became disconnected from my-self and depressed. Eventually, as the thread that kept my marriage together began to fray, I became resentful.

I had to learn the hard way that although being a mum and a wife was an important part of my life, it was not all of who I was. I was more. Much more. I was a woman with my own secret desires and dreams, longing to live a life filled with excitement and spontaneity; a woman who wanted to leave her mark on the world by living her life with purpose and passion; a woman who at the end of her life wanted to be able to look back and smile at having lived an extraordinary life.

Through trust in her Self, Ghania radiates completeness.

To truly live an extraordinary life, I realised that I needed to make a commitment to take care of my own needs before the needs of others. This was a concept that had previously seemed abhorrent to me. The truth, I came to learn, was that I could not expect others to do for me what I was unwilling to do for my-self.

As I practiced doing small things for my-self, be it taking the time out to read a book or enjoy a cup of tea in the winter sun, I became more comfortable at spending lengthier periods of time looking after my own needs and desires. I allowed my-self to nourish my soul with the activities that gave me joy, and in the process I emerged a complete woman rather than the incomplete woman I had for far too long felt I was. A surprising side-effect of the process of becoming 'whole' was the rebirth of my ability to trust my-self to look after my own needs and desires. In trusting my-self, I re-embraced the belief that others, too, were worthy of my trust.

Looking after my-self and practising self-love and trust allowed me to become self-*centred* – where the emphasis is on being centred within my-self as opposed to becoming *self*-centred, where the emphasis is on being selfish to the detriment of all and everybody else.

Self-love and becoming self-*centred* dictates that we, as individuals, invest in our own emotional health and wellbeing before we seek to invest in the wellbeing of others. Only when we respect, honour, love, trust and appreciate ourselves are we truly able to do the same for others and thus sustain enduring, loving relationships.

Embracing self-love and becoming self-*centred* also means being gentle with ourselves as we embrace new and better ways of living. Inevitably, all of us slip and fall at times as we embark on a journey of conscious change and extraordinary living. How you respond is within your power. You can choose to remain on the ground, beating yourself up about your undesirable behaviour and feeling sorry for yourself, OR you can choose to gently pick yourself up and keep on going, one small step at a time.

I know there's been many a time when I've caught myself slipping into old behaviours. Rather than beat myself up (like I would have in the past), I now choose to become consciously aware of how I can avoid making the same slip-up the next time I am faced with a similar situation. We are all human and as such we are all vulnerable to making mistakes. The trick, I believe, is to embrace our mistakes and use them as a vehicle for even greater learning and self-awareness.

Control What You Can and Surrender to What You Can't

'There is only one way to happiness, and that is to cease worrying about things which are beyond the power of our will'

~ *Epictetus*

Most women I meet have a not so secret desire to be in control – of themselves, their feelings, their husbands/partners and their life in general. Two things that most of us shy away from being in control of, though, are our thoughts and our subsequent actions. This is quite interesting given that they are the only two things we truly have the power to control.

We may believe that we can control other parts of our lives, but seriously, how many of us are, for example, able to control our partners *AND* have a happy fulfilling relationship? It's only when we accept the other person for who they are that we can truly flourish in a relationship.

It's only when we accept the other person for who they are that we can truly flourish in a relationship.

Just to be clear, I am not in any way or form advocating the acceptance of emotionally or physically abusive behaviour by your partner towards you or your children – be it gambling or any other active addiction, chronic infidelity or physical and/or emotional abuse. A man or woman who is unable to respect you and/or your children's emotional and physical wellbeing does not deserve to be in a relationship with you. It's that simple, that black and white. And you owe it to your-self and your children to get out of that relationship.

In a relationship where none of the above factors are present, the best that we can do is to be in control of our-selves. This simply means to be in control of our thoughts and our actions, including our responses to others and life in general.

I spent far too many years living in a reactionary state, feeling I had no control over my thoughts and no power to control how I reacted to certain events. The concept of taking the time to dismiss the thoughts that did not serve me and consciously choose thoughts that did serve me, and to reflect and respond from a place of self-*centredness,* was unknown to me.

Through my training as an NLP practitioner and human behaviour specialist, I discovered that the only person I could control was my-self. I learnt strategies that enabled me to choose my thoughts, to sit in my discomfort, reflect on the situation and choose the best response. I went from being reactionary to cultivating the power to respond.

Just as important is the power to surrender to the things we cannot control. Quite often it is easy to become overwhelmed with all the detail that constitute 'life' – our dreams and passions, our worries, our daily To-Do lists and our goals. The more attached we become to the outcome, the more we hold on and the greater mental and emotional energy we expend.

As Epictetus, Greek sage and Stoic philosopher quoted almost 2,000 years ago, 'There is only one way to happiness, and that is to cease worrying about things which are beyond the power of our will.' Personal suffering arises from trying to control what is uncontrollable, a lesson I have had to learn many times over. Obsessing over every detail of my never diminishing To-Do list, while yearning for the achievement of my personal dreams and goals, resulted in me suffering from that modern phenomena – 'stress'. By learning the art of surrender, I have allowed myself to embrace my humanness, to accept quite consciously that there are many things in my life over which I have little or no control and to trust that when the time is right my dreams and goals will manifest. By trusting God and surrendering to His plan for me, I have learnt many lessons – faith, patience, hope, love, forgiveness and acceptance.

Surrendering also means relinquishing the expectation that others will behave the way you want them to behave. Rather than agonise over your lack of ability to control how your husband, ex-husband, best friend or family members behave, become the change you desire in others. Behave how you desire them to behave. By doing this, you gift yourself with the ability to live more consciously and to be truly in a position of influence, rather than be a victim of circumstance.

Surrendering means relinquishing the expectation that others will behave the way you want them to behave.

Everything in life is about energy, including the energy we put out toward others. Most of our communication is non-verbal and our message is inherently affected by the energy that we exude. As feeling beings, we have the ability to pick up on whether someone is approaching us from a place of love and empathy or from a place of resentment, hate or judgment. By changing the energy we reflect towards others, we can significantly change the nature and the outcome of our interactions. My relationship with my ex-husband was strained and draining when I approached him from a place of judgment and resentment. It was only when I was able to release my resentment and judgment that I was able to finally have a relationship with him that is, I believe, now built on mutual respect.

Shhhh ...
The Secret: Masculine-Feminine Energy Balance

'If a woman can only succeed by emulating men, I think it is a great loss and not a success. The aim is not only for a woman to succeed but to keep her womanhood and let her womanhood influence society.'

~ *Suzanne Brogger*

If your childhood was anything like mine, chances are that you were raised in a family where male and female roles were clearly defined; your mother probably did no work outside of the home and your father was the sole provider.

Traditionally, men were supposed to go to work and be the providers, while women were expected to stay at home and take care of the children and the household duties. The second half of the twentieth century, however, was characterised by much sociological change, particularly in the realm of intimate relationships and marriage. During World War II, women entered the work force and never completely returned to 'traditional' roles. In the 1960's and 70's, men began to get in touch with their inner feminine. They exhibited a more loving, gentle and sensitive side to their nature and embraced external characteristics of the feminine, including long hair, flowing colourful clothes and an affinity with nature and music. Meanwhile, the feminist movement was at its peak. Women placed an emphasis on their financial and political independence, sought direction and prestige, and strengthened both their education and their careers. They openly magnified their inner masculine and became more independent and assertive than their mothers had been.

Amidst this rush for equality, the dynamics of intimate relationships changed. Consequently, the rules that once applied to our parents and grandparents no longer apply to us, and this has left our generation without a clear set of relationship guidelines.

Men often complain that too many women have become masculine, too independent and self-sufficient, and emotionally guarded. They lament that the modern woman frowns upon good old fashioned chivalry; that they are often confused about how to treat a woman; and that they feel dispensable.

Feminism was about demonstrating that women were as capable as men to be educated, goal oriented and successful.

Women, on the other hand, complain that too many men have become afraid of, or are intimated by, successful women and fail to give women the support they need. More common is the complaint that men have taken on feminine traits such as expecting the woman to become the provider and take care of them financially. It is also not uncommon for men to expect women to pursue them, initiate the relationship or to pay when they go out on dates.

Is it any wonder that men and women are confused when it comes to intimate relationships and that marriage rates have been steadily declining since the 1970's, while divorce rates have been steadily increasing?

As wonderful as feminism has been for women and society in general, I believe it was not intended to masculinise women or threaten the institution of marriage. Rather, feminism was about demonstrating that women were as capable as men to be educated, goal oriented and successful. It was about affording both sexes the same opportunities rather than declaring that men and women were created one and the same.

The fact is that women and men were created differently and each one of us has been instilled with our own unique essence or balance of masculine and feminine energy. Men and women can possess both masculine and feminine energy and aren't limited to one type of energy based on their gender. Neither energy types is superior to the other, and indeed masculine and feminine energy complement and are drawn to each other like opposing forces of a magnet.

Masculine energy is driven, pragmatic, functional and focused. It is characterised by rational, direct, practical, action-oriented and assertive qualities. The masculine energy is the energy of power, physical strength, decision making and mental strength. A predominance of masculine energy is generally associated with men. Men who have a predominantly masculine energy want and need to feel in control without (generally) needing to be controlling. They have an inherent need to offer solutions and have the mental strength to remain focused on a problem until it is solved. The masculine energy loves to get things done and feels free when a task or purpose has been accomplished. Flowing on from this, men generally get fulfilment from a relationship where they are the solution providers most of the time and where they are given the opportunity to provide, protect and accomplish.

In contrast, feminine energy is more receptive, flowing, nurturing, supportive and gentle. Some of the greatest gifts of the feminine are depth of feeling, intuition and compassion. The feminine is humanitarian and creative (the artist within each of us). Just as a predominance of masculine energy is associated with men, a predominance of feminine energy is associated with women. Women who have a predominantly feminine energy want to be heard rather than just be given solutions. They feel respected when their feelings are cherished and have an inherent desire to be filled with love. In fact, the feminine is most inspired by love and connection.

Although all of us have aspects of both masculine and feminine energies in our personalities, we all have a preference for one energy type. Men naturally gravitate towards masculine energy and women towards feminine energy. Spending too much time in an opposing energy can leave one feeling disconnected, stressed and anxious. Generally, to enhance feelings of internal balance and connectedness, the masculine energy in a woman should be her less dominant energy and the feminine energy in the man should be his less dominant energy[4].

---

4 This is a generalisation that applies to the average man and woman. There are men (heterosexual or otherwise) who have a predominantly feminine essence just as there are women who have a predominantly masculine essence. To simplify the masculine feminine energy balance, I have chosen to focus on the most common case of masculine energy (being a man with a predominantly masculine energy) and the most common case of feminine energy (being a woman with a predominantly feminine energy).

The unique thing about a romantic relationship is the balance of masculine and feminine energy that flows back and forth between the couple. Because passion is created by the polarity in energy, relationships work best when the man is predominately masculine in his energy and the woman is predominantly feminine in her energy[5].

Although our grandparents had clearly defined roles that allowed them to remain in their masculine energy (for men) or their feminine energy (for women), the changes in society and gender roles in general has caused an imbalance in masculine/feminine energy. This imbalance is of critical importance on both a personal level and an interpersonal level because an imbalance of masculine/feminine energy can upset the polarity in energy, create tension in your relationship and have an adverse effect on the sexual passion between you and your partner.

As a woman you will feel happier, less stressed and more balanced if you spend most of your time or remain in your feminine energy. The challenge for the modern woman, however, is being able to reconcile her feminine essence with her desire for independence and purpose in life. As fulfilling as motherhood can be, many of us aren't happy with being simply a mum or wife. We want our contribution to the world to extend beyond our home front, but may be hesitant about the effect this could have on our mothering role and on our intimacy with our partner, be it emotional or sexual.

The challenge for the modern woman is being able to reconcile her feminine essence with her desire for independence and purpose in life.

For the working woman (whether single or attached), the challenge is extended further. Generally, women believe that they have to adopt a masculine persona or be predominantly masculine in their energy to be

5 Again, I am generalising by referring to the most common type of relationship which consists of a man with a natural predominance of masculine energy and a woman with a natural predominance of feminine energy. Relationships can work just as well, for example, between a man with a predominantly feminine energy and a woman with a predominantly masculine energy because the polarity in energy is maintained.

accomplished and respected in the business world. This belief tends to be more pronounced in industries that were traditionally the exclusive realm of men. There is no doubt that women can be as accomplished and as successful as men; they have the ability to access their masculine energy to stay focused, accomplish tasks and achieve a desired outcome at work. However, residing in her masculine energy for too long can adversely affect a woman's mental and physical health, resulting in increased stress and disease. An emphasis on her masculine energy will also put a dampener on her intimate relationship because men who are strong in their masculine energy are inherently drawn to a woman whose essence resides in her feminine energy. To put it simply, men find feminine women irresistible, and a feminine woman is more likely to attract a man who is masculine and more capable of fulfilling his role of protector and provider.

Similarly, approaching the business world from your feminine energy will provide you with better results, less stress and a feeling of internal balance and harmony. If you approach men at work from your masculine, they are more likely to unconsciously regard you as one of the boys and treat you accordingly – this often means that you evoke within them the masculine desire to win (against you!). Approaching them from your feminine energy will evoke in them an unconscious desire to help and support you to get to where you want to be. Some of the most successful women are in tune with their feminine energy and are comfortable in being there.

If, however, you are required to reside in your masculine energy most of the time while at work, being able to return to your feminine energy once you exit the work environment is essential for internal balance and harmony and is one of the key components for a happier relationship. Achieving this may be as simple as allowing yourself the luxury of a facial or day spa treatment, hanging out with your girlfriends or taking some time out to listen to relaxing or uplifting music on the way home.

In an intimate relationship, being aware of what energy you are accessing and when you are accessing it are key. If you are in 'doing mode' or are called upon to make decisions, you are residing in your masculine energy. If you're in 'being mode' and are focused on the experience and how it feels, rather than the outcome, you are accessing your feminine energy.

The problem I found from my own experience of having been married almost a decade is that we modern women are generally more in tune with our masculine energy than our feminine energy. We are skilled at telling our partners what to do and exactly how to do it, and when he fails to do it exactly as we specified, we are quick to jump in and take over. We tell ourselves that we can do 'it' better, but meanwhile the resentment at having to 'do it all' is slowly building.

Although the onus is on the man in the relationship to prove that he is able to protect and provide, the secret to a happy, fulfilling relationship may be as simple as allowing yourself the luxury of remaining in your feminine energy and allowing him the opportunity to dwell in his masculine. Enjoy having a man romance you and look after you. Let him open doors for you, pull out chairs and pay the bill. Let him organise the whole event while you simply enjoy the experience. Allowing your partner to take on the masculine role while you revel in your feminine energy doesn't make you any less of a woman, but it does allow the man in your life to fulfil his desire to provide and protect you. This applies whether the man in question is someone you've just started dating or your husband of ten years.

Allowing yourself to come from your feminine, and being confident in your ability to do so, will enable you to get things done much more effectively and more enjoyably than coming purely from your masculine energy. Because the man in your life will respond more favourably to your feminine energy, approaching him from your feminine energy will mean that he is more likely to really listen to you and give you what you desire.

One of the gems I uncovered in my own quest for answers is that most often a man is only truly fulfilled when the woman in his life is safe, happy and has had her desires met by him. Telling a man how you feel – 'When you answered the phone during our talk, I felt hurt and unimportant' rather than 'Next time, don't pick up the phone when we are talking!'– will provide you with a better outcome because it allows a man to fulfil his inherent masculine desire to protect and care for you. This requires less energy on your

> *Most often a man is only truly fulfilled when the woman in his life is safe, happy and has had her desires met by him.*

part and allows the intimacy in your relationship to be preserved.

Indeed, understanding and capitalising on the differences between men and women and their unique energies are some of the best kept secrets to a fulfilling, passionate and exciting relationship where a foundation of honesty, mutual trust, understanding, empathy and respect is present.

By embracing self-love and understanding the dynamics of masculine/feminine energy balance, you too will be able to create and sustain extraordinary relationships filled with love, passion, excitement and mutual understanding. Below are strategies I wish to share with you that can assist you on your own journey towards an extraordinary life.

Suggestions to Help You Live Extraordinarily by Incorporating This Guidance into Your Life

 ## *Create a Surrender Box/Journal*

A tool that I love to suggest is the Surrender Box/Journal. By creating and using a Surrender Box or Journal, you allow yourself to let go of your concerns and desires so that they can be taken care of for you – by God/Life/Universe/Law of Attraction. The process is simple: Create a 'surrender slip' by writing what you would like to happen on a piece of plain or fancy paper. This can be the realisation of a particular dream or goal, or the resolution of a pressing worry or concern. Place the surrender slip in your Surrender Box, or paste it into your Surrender Journal, and give yourself permission to surrender the outcome of that dream or worry to a greater power. This allows you to free up space in your mind so that you are living each moment more consciously.

You can have a lot of fun with this. Decorate your Surrender Box or Journal with your favourite colours, quotes and pictures. Use different types and colours of paper for your surrender slips. Every so often, pull out your Surrender Box or Journal and read through your surrender slips – you'll be pleasantly surprised at just how many of your worries have resolved themselves and how many of your dreams or desires have been granted.

✿ *Embrace all of you*

One of the things that come far too easily to women is self-criticism. Most of us are familiar with that inner critic that tells us we are not thin enough, pretty enough, accomplished enough, perfect enough or _____ (*insert word*) enough! Often times, our inner critic is conveniently, and not surprisingly, reflected by an outer critic: the lover that will never accept you for who you truly are; the 'friend' who constantly puts you down or can do whatever you can do better, bigger and faster.

The list of internal and external criticisms can be endless … but only if we allow it to be. By accepting these criticisms, we allow our inner and outer critics to steal away our self-confidence and our zest for life. To combat this, we need to embrace and love ourselves for the wonderful, loving, compassionate women we are. The greatest gifts that you can give to yourself are the gifts of self-love and acceptance.

Today, consciously decide to love yourself fully. Stand in front of a mirror and tell the woman looking back that you love and honour her. Your body, regardless of its shape or size, has supported you through your journey in life – through your trials and tribulations, your joys and accomplishments. It may have carried a child(ren), survived the impact of an accident, or supported you through marathons or hours of strenuous physical training. It is your sacred temple. Love it in all its splendour and embrace it, not despite of, but rather for all of its imperfections.

Similarly, embrace other non-physical parts of yourself that you have spent years dismissing or criticising. Accept your imperfections and consciously decide to be gentle on yourself. Life becomes much more interesting when we banish our critics and abandon our quest for perfection. We begin to take life less seriously and allow ourselves to have fun. By practising self-love and acceptance, we give ourselves permission to experiment and experience more of what life has to offer.

 ## *Consciously approach your man from your feminine*

The wonderful thing about masculine and feminine energy is that if you approach the man in your life from your feminine energy rather than your masculine, you will inspire him into action and into caring for you in the way you truly desire.

If you're reading this book, chances are that you are a woman with a predominantly feminine energy and that the man in your life most likely has a predominantly masculine energy. As I have previously covered, the masculine is directive. Accordingly, when you tell a man what to do, you are approaching him from your masculine energy and by doing so you will inadvertently push him away. The average man, whose dominant energy is masculine, will generally resist a woman's directives and be repelled by her telling him what needs to be done, when and how.

To inspire your man into action, approach him from your feminine by expressing how you feel about something rather than telling him what to do with it/about it. Something as simple as 'It makes me really happy and proud when you maintain the lawn' (accompanied with a big appreciative smile) will inspire him into action, while whingeing and complaining that he never mows the lawn on time will make him less willing to please you. The masculine loves to provide for and protect the feminine. The masculine also loves to win, and most often the masculine's most prized possession is your smile and your genuine appreciation. Try it out for a week and take note of the effect your new approach has on your relationship and your life.

GET YOUR EXTRAORDINARY
FREE GIFT BONUS

Ghania Dib is kindly offering a **FREE BONUS GIFT**
to all readers of this book.

7 Secrets to Igniting Your Deeper Love Connection

A free video series and weekly
Love Connection and Relationship Tips.

Simply visit the web page below and
follow the directions to directly download
7 Secrets to Igniting Your Deeper Love Connection.

www.philosophylivelovethrive.com

'We are each born knowing how to
communicate with all sentient beings.
Our souls hold this innate wisdom ...
Remembering our connection with animals
and understanding that unity with them
helps us become awakened and whole.'

Asia Voight

Asia is an internationally-known Animal Communicator, Intuitive Counsellor, author, teacher and inspirational speaker who has worked with over 50,000 animals in the last fourteen years. Asia's work has been featured on ABC, NBC and Fox TV as well as countless radio interviews like the Rick Lamb Show, Hay House Radio and Olympic dressage rider Jane Savoie's teleseminar. She has graced the covers of many publications, such as *Brava* and *Women Magazine,* and the front pages of the *Wisconsin State Journal* and the *Fitchburg Star* with her amazing personal story and words of animal wisdom.

Speaking in front of thousands of animal lovers, Asia is a popular keynote speaker for countless events like the Midwest Horse Fair® in Madison, Wisconsin, where she has delighted audiences with her on-the-spot personal readings, humour and warmth.

A popular teacher in her Animal Communication workshops, Asia generously shares her skills by gently guiding course participants on how to connect with one's own animal companions through exercises and guided meditations. Described as unforgettable and life-altering, Asia's week-long trips to the gorgeous destinations of the Bahamas, Dominican Republic and Costa Rica give participants a chance to swim, snorkel and, yes, communicate with wild dolphins, whales and turtles!

Asia's work also includes healings for people: Past-life regressions, life readings, and chakra and vibrational healings. Watch for Asia's upcoming book, *Burned Back to Spirit: Awakening Your Intuitive Powers by Way of One Woman's Near Death Experience.*

Awakening Your Natural Ability to Heal Through Animal Communication

ASIA VOIGHT

We are each born knowing how to communicate with all sentient beings. Our souls hold this innate wisdom. This type of communication has many names: gut feeling, inner knowing, intuition, hunch, sixth sense, divine connection, sensing, psychic ability and telepathy. However, these are merely different words for expressing an energetic union with another being. Since all of life is energy, we can learn to heighten our abilities and tune into this energy so that we may be blessed to hear messages from our animal companions. In *The Map, Finding the Magic and Meaning in the Story of Your Life*, Colette Baron-Reid states, 'If you're willing to enter into a partnership with Spirit and allow your imagination to be ignited and inspired, you'll be amazed by the results.' Once you know how to use this in-born ability, you'll be able to communicate with nature, angels, spirit guides, ascended masters and loved ones who have passed.

Talking with animals may seem fanciful, when in reality the ability to communicate with them is essential to the well-being of both ourselves and our animals. Holding conversations with my animals saved my life. After a near-fatal car accident, my dog, Makeba, and my horse, Magic, helped me heal. Having the aid of your animals, who know you better than anyone, can help guide you through life's challenges. Whether you are looking to change careers, leave a bad relationship or need help figuring out what is next in your life, the animals are there to assist you.

As a Professional Animal Communicator, most people call on me to help them resolve emotional and behavioural issues in their animal companions. A simple conversation usually takes care of these issues. Once the more obvious issue is resolved, the secret, more profound reason for my being invited is revealed. There is something more that wants to be known from these intuitive conversations, and it is almost always about the animal's person. Through telepathic communication animals bring forward information to help their human heal. Animals are wise beings aware of the 'goings on' in their home, their person's lives and even at their work. Although animals are physically different from humans, they hold the same spiritual, emotional and energetic substances we do and are therefore able to bring forth information we may be unaware of. They take their jobs very seriously.

Through telepathic communication animals bring forward information to help their human heal.

In my own experience, several of my animals told me that their life's mission was to help me work through fear, denial, illusions and defensiveness until I became more emotionally and spiritually whole. Such was the case when my horse, Magic, told me about my past life pain and its negative effects on us. He knew I would be freer to hear the voice of spirit, angels and animals more clearly by helping me break through false beliefs. Your animals desire to do the same for you. Are you willing to honour their gifts and find greater freedom in your life?

Even if you didn't communicate with animals as a child or you don't think you are able, that's okay. It is never too late to learn. After all, it is not really about learning, but remembering ... remembering who we are, remembering how we are all interconnected and remembering our past lives.

In my case, remembering came through a car accident in which I travelled to the other side during a near-death experience. Later, I would journey several more times out of my broken body to learn from the ascended masters, angels and guides, who were there to help me.

Remembering Through Fire

In 1987, after my twenty-third birthday, during the long drive from my home state of Wisconsin to Florida, a semi-trailer crashed into my van. In an instant a raging gasoline-bred fire held me prisoner. I struggled to escape by pulling on the van's warped doors. None of them opened and black smoke poured in through the cracks. About to give up, my luminous guardian angel appeared before my eyes. Guiding me out a narrow window I could not have fit through, I lived, but over seventy-two per cent of my body was severely burned. The ER doctor gave me little to no chance for survival.

Months later, the doctor's prediction came true. In the ICU my lungs collapsed and I died. Met on the other side by ascended masters, representatives of God, they gave me various healing and spiritual lessons. One of them concerned intuitive communication. They showed me that telepathy is our soul's language. I had turned off my telepathic abilities years before, and yet immediately on the other side I knew how to share a mind-to-mind and heart-to-heart connection with the ascended masters. I didn't have to take a class to learn how to hear them. I knew how because my soul knew how. Intuitive connection with animals is nothing we have to learn, but rather, simply remember. The first step is accepting in your heart that connection and healing with animals is possible.

Intuitive connection with animals is nothing we have to learn, but rather, simply remember.

For many of us who did communicate with animals as children and then 'lost' this ability, there are multiple reasons for this disconnection: among them abuse, fear, wanting to be seen as normal, lack of support or being teased. In our society, unlike many native or aboriginal tribes that reach out to the animals for assistance, we've been taught to distrust our gut feelings and separate ourselves from them. In *Teen Psychic: Exploring Your Intuitive Spiritual Powers,* Julie Tallard Johnson states, 'The practice of claiming our intuition is really about tapping into our inner wisdom – claiming our life fully, all of who we are.' When we compromise ourselves by trying to fit in or please others, we push away our souls' inner knowing, rejecting who we are.

Remembering our connection with animals and understanding that unity with them helps us become awakened and whole. This incredible unity creates a ripple beyond those directly involved and goes on to positively impact the entire planet as well.

> *'All things share the same breath – the beast, the tree, the man. The air shares its spirit with all the life it supports. If all the beasts were gone, man would die from loneliness of spirit; for whatsoever happens to the beast, happens to the man. All things are connected. Whatever befalls the earth, befalls the sons of earth.'*
> ~ *Chief Seattle*

Sending Signals: Three Paths to Healing with Animals

There are three ways in which animals signal the need for us to heal: 1) taking on our physical and/or emotional issues; 2) acting out because of a current issue; 3) and acting out because of a past life issue. Animals, of course, have their own experiences and can get sick due to their own issues or their own naturally ageing bodies. Yet, I've often witnessed how they become ill or act out because they recognised our need to heal. Animals can be born with their own quirky behaviours and it doesn't necessarily mean they are sending you a message to heal or that they are acting out. Acting out might mean your animal is suddenly behaving differently to their normal behaviour. It is always best to start a healing journey with your animal companion by asking them: Are you acting this way to send me a message?

1.   *Animals Taking on Our Issues*

My sessions with clients usually start with them wanting to know what is wrong with their animal friend. They witness a physical or emotional problem in their cat, dog or horse. What they do not realise is that often their animal has taken on their issue. The way for both of them to heal is rooted in the person awakening to the reality that we are all connected.

In order for an authentic healing to take place, the human in this relationship must come to some understanding of the underlying reality of interconnectedness. It is essential to realise that the animal is acting as a mirror in a very personal and dynamic way. Are you willing to change self-defeating behaviours to help you and your animal companion heal?

In *Animal Talk,* Penelope Smith states, 'Animals can get caught up in their humans' imbalances because of their dependency and also their deep desire to serve and help their human friends. Sickness can result when the animal attempts to heal or take away human misery or to mirror it.'

An example of an animal taking on its person's issue occurred during a communication session with a woman named Colleen and her dog, Scout. They made an appointment at a holistic veterinary clinic where I occasionally work. I had never met them before.

'I want to know what is wrong with my dog,' Colleen said. 'She is having indigestion problems ... burping excessively and throwing up. The veterinarians can't figure it out.'

While she spoke, Scout, a large white mixed breed sat politely with intense eyes. Next to her, Colleen's husband, Bill, silently stroked Scout's head.

'Scout, when you're ready.' I waved my hand in the air to get her attention. 'Please send me words, pictures, feelings or body sensations of what you want to express. And Scout, whatever you want to start with is fine,' I said to her.

Scout's ears pricked upright as her eyes locked with mine. When I heard Scout's words in my mind, I immediately repeated them out loud.

'Burning,' I heard her say. 'My throat and stomach are burning.'

'Okay, very good. I was told you are having indigestion,' I said. 'Tell me more about why that is happening.'

I could feel Scout's heart breaking as she turned to look at Colleen. 'She drinks liquid that burns her throat and stomach and I feel the burning, too. Please ask her to stop drinking the poison.'

Bill's eyes bulged and his face flushed as he leaned forward in his chair. He turned toward Colleen and put one hand on his hip. Colleen's voice jumped an octave as she giggled, 'Oh, she must mean the cola I drink,' she said while vigorously nodding her head. Then turning to Scout, she said, 'Right baby? Is that what you mean?'

'No,' said Scout sadly. 'The clear liquid you put in your cola.'

Colleen started crying and then Scout took a deep sigh and relaxed on the cool tiled floor. Finally, her message had been heard. 'I'll get help, Scouttie, I promise. I haven't been able to quit drinking on my own or even for Bill. Now that I know it's hurting you too, I'll stop.'

Scout had taken on Colleen's pain first to help her body not take the full damage of being a heavy drinker and secondly to say, 'If you can't love yourself enough to change, I'm hoping you will do it for me.' Since Colleen did not hear her dog telepathically, Scout tried to bring attention to the issue with clear physical symptoms. Scout's pain eventually led them to seek my help, which revealed the core problem. Scout and Colleen both healed. Fortunately, you don't need an intuitive such as myself to have the truth of your animal's issues revealed to you. You can simply look at your animal companion or visualise them in your mind's eye while taking a deep breath and ask them: 'Are you taking on any of my issues?' You might hear, see, feel or sense in your body a 'yes' or 'no' answer.

> *Animals can lead us out of the maze of pain, victimhood and false beliefs we have about ourselves.*

Animals can lead us out of the maze of pain, victimhood and false beliefs we have about ourselves. Sometimes the animals might be the only beings in your life you trust, especially if others have betrayed or disappointed you. Many of my clients feel they can rely on no one except their animal companions. We can use this trust to fully tune into them and listen to what they have to say.

2.   *Animals Acting Out to Bring Healing*

> *'No living creature defines a life of devotion and loyalty better than the dog. When we take the time to thoughtfully observe the lives of animals, these qualities speak to our spirits, inspire us, warn us, heal us.'*
>
> ~ *Susan Chernak McElroy, Animals as Guides for the Soul*

The other way in which animals help us heal is by acting out until we figure out what is really going on. When we adopt an animal into our lives, we imagine a deep, loving and easy relationship. Most often that scene plays out, but what if it doesn't? If your animal friend has begun to act differently, take note of your own life. Did the behavioural issue start around the same time that you went through some personal crisis? Maybe you felt lost, hit rock bottom and you didn't know what to do next. Your animal friend heard your call for help and stepped forward by acting out and getting you to pay attention to something. If you are not hearing your animal telepathically, or if you choose to ignore what he is telling you, he will definitely find a way to get you to listen!

Adopting my mixed breed dog, Makeba, seven months after my car accident might not have seemed like the best choice at the time. But it wouldn't take long for her to teach me an important lesson about power.

When about to leave the animal shelter in Appleton, Wisconsin, without a dog, at the last moment I spotted a grey, black-and-white puppy standing near the receptionist's desk. Bending over the counter to take a peek at this little ball of fur, I felt a jolt in my heart when I looked at her.

If you are not hearing your animal telepathically, or if you choose to ignore what he is telling you, he will definitely find a way to get you to listen!

'That little dog belongs to someone back here, right?' I asked the staff member.

'No,' the woman brightly said. 'She's not taken. She's just behind the desk for special attention.'

'She's exactly the type of dog I'm looking for!'

Swallowing hard, tears welled up as I peered down into her six-month-old furry face. She looked exactly like Bijou, my dog who was killed in my fiery crash a mere seven months prior. Gazing into her fuzzy face brought back memories of my van, crushed and burned by the semi-truck. That van had contained everything I owned and had been my home for months while I travelled. Aware of the pricking and tingling sensation in my burnt legs since the accident, I distracted myself by picking up the puppy. The fire had taken everything from me: skin, hair, money, body, home and my dog. Broke, weak, disabled and powerless, I had given up on life. Crazy-hopeful, I took her home and named her 'Makeba'. I anticipated that this new puppy would revitalise me and give me a reason to live.

Once home, I noticed that the intuitive hearing I had shut down as a teenager started coming back. Word by word, feeling by feeling, she kept sending messages to me. If I didn't hear her correctly, she would stare at me and stomp her paw. Going through the normal desires of a dog, 'treat' or 'toy' simply did not work. 'Sound out the obvious of what I'm doing,' she would say. 'If I'm walking toward the door say, You want to go outside? That will get your mind flowing and make it easier for you to hear me.'

We certainly needed communication help when it came to our daily walks. Before sunrise I would take Makeba for her walk, if you could call it that. We went out early so no one could see us. Gripping the leather leash with white knuckles, I would hold on and lean backwards like a water-skier to counterbalance her strength. She would lunge forward, digging her back feet into the earth like a jackrabbit. Repeatedly, I came close to being dragged across the concrete and through the brush, which my fragile, thin-skinned body could not have taken. I tried scolding her, but she just looked at me with a sly grin.

'Why aren't you walking nicely?' I asked her.

'You have no power.'

'That's not what I asked you.'

'But that's the answer,' she said.

'If you would just walk nicely, all our problems would be solved!' I replied.

'No, you have a lot of problems and they're about your lack of power. I am not the only one in your life dragging you all over the place.'

'Whatever,' I answered tersely. 'I'm taking you to a dog training class and you'll see who has the problem.'

The next week we enrolled in a beginners' dog training class. But by the end of the class, my clothes were soaked with sweat and I drooped in exhaustion. My frustration soon gave way to a wave of tears as Makeba had lunged at every single dog and person in class.

'You'll be asked to leave if you don't get your dog under control,' the teacher yelled out.

'What? Kicked out? I need help with her. That's why I'm here,' I replied.

'It's not her, it's you. You're a wimp with your dog,' she said, taking hold of the lead rope. Getting Makeba's attention, she then said in a deep, clear and powerful voice, 'Sit.' Instantaneously, Makeba sat down, turned her head and smiled at me. 'Practice that and I'll see you next week,' said the instructor firmly as she handed the leash back to me. I was thunderstruck by Makeba's obedient performance and sly smile, for it was just as if she were saying, 'I told you so.'

For weeks we practised at dog training class and at home. Allowing my communication skills to blossom, I sent telepathic pictures to her during our training of what I wanted. I made commands with power. It worked, and seven weeks later we finished in first place during a class competition. This new energy also gave me the power I needed to make other changes in my life, like finally letting go of an unhealthy relationship with a friend.

The next time your animal companion is acting out consider what she may be trying to tell you. What does her behaviour bring up in you? Her behaviour is pointing to some shared dynamic. Take some notes and then follow your animal companion around by 'sounding out' what the obvious physical signals are that she is giving you. This simple exercise will get your mind open and flowing in the right direction for telepathic communication. After practicing this method for a few minutes, find a relaxing position and ask for a word, picture or feeling from her.

3.   *Animals Healing Our Past Lives*

> *'Virgil (my horse) is my salvation and my therapist;*
> *he listens to me and rejuvenates me.'*
>
> ~ *Judy A. Brown, Contributor,*
> ***The Healing Touch of Horses, Editor A. B Llewellyn***

The third way animals can help us heal is through past lives. Past lives that come forward can be a life that both of you have lived together or a separate life time. Raised in a conservative Christian home, the concept of past lives was not a part of my upbringing. Even so, as a child I often had an odd feeling of déjà vu and saw people's faces change and observed scenes from different time periods moving around them. Initially, I didn't understand this and because of my religious upbringing, I felt fearful seeing this.

During my near-death experience, the ascended masters spoke to me about 'other lives' as they are not exactly past lives, since they are affecting us now. When a past life is still affecting us, an unresolved or unhealed issue will present itself again and again until healed. (I go into detail on this in my upcoming book, *Burned Back to Spirit, Awakening Your Intuitive Powers by Way of One Woman's Near-Death Experience*.) One day I discovered that my horse, Magic, knew about my other lifetimes. Most animals know this information and want to share it with their humans. Past lives can be shown to help you heal or to show forgotten talents. Magic showed me how to heal the hidden shame and guilt I'd been carrying in my energetic body for eons. He also showed me how love can heal any pain.

During my near-death experience, the ascended masters spoke to me about 'other lives' as they are not exactly past lives, since they are affecting us now.

'Stop flipping your head around,' I said to Magic. We were riding in the dusty indoor arena at the horse farm where he was boarded. But instead of stopping, he kicked out his front legs and flipped his black and white mane from side to side. 'This is dangerous. Stop it!' I snapped. He jerked his head down, yanking the reins right out of my hands. Scared and bewildered, I quickly pulled my black boots from the stirrups and flipped my right leg over his back, dismounting. Upset, with tears streaming down my face, I was unable to clearly communicate with him. I needed to calm myself down. Taking a deep breath and feeling my feet solidly planted on the ground, I centred myself by visualising a cord of light going down from my feet into the centre of the earth. I then asked Magic some questions.

'Okay, is the problem your saddle? This is the forty-eighth saddle, by the way, that I have tried for you.'

'No,' he flatly responded.

'Thank God,' I said, letting out a huge sigh.

'I didn't say the saddle was great, I am just saying I wasn't tossing my head because of the saddle.'

'Oh. What is it then?'

'You've got to really let go in your mind for this one. You should go home and lie down. It's not what you're expecting,' he said kindly.

'You're scaring me,' I replied, feeling my heart beat up into my throat.

'Can't you just tell me why you're acting this way right now?'

'When you sit on me, I can feel an unhealed energy flowing in your body. These are energies from different lifetimes where guilt, fear and shame consumed you and you died never completing the healing cycle. Go home and connect with me from there. I'll show you.'

Slumped in frustration, I headed home. Once there I turned my phone off, went into my bedroom, lowered the lights, played soothing music and laid down. I focused on my desire to communicate with Magic as I visualised his face in my mind's eye. I asked for help from beings of light, relaxed all my body parts, breathed slowly, trusted that he would connect with me and looked up in my mind's eye as I saw him coming toward me.

Suddenly, I saw us walking down a hill and across a wooden bridge. Reaching the other side, Magic turned into a solid white horse with smaller, more refined features. The scenery around us transformed as large trees appeared alongside a dirt road leading to a large stone barn ahead. Looking down at my body, I noticed that I had become an older male with a pudgy belly, wearing a uniform. Magic graciously pranced by me as I joyously walked him into the barn. The tall stone and wood-beamed stable held about fifty horses. All of the horses living in the barn were bay or black in colour and quite stocky. Magic's bright white coat

His kind and willing demeanour cast a net of true magic, filling me with deep love for him.

and refined movements stood out, making him seem otherworldly. His kind and willing demeanour cast a net of true magic, filling me with deep love for him.

My reverie was interrupted as a guard standing by the large front door called out, 'The king is here!'

Everyone quickly lined up and bent over their feet in a slight bow to His Majesty. Then the white-haired king halted right in front of me.

'Have you finished the bit?' he inquired.

'Yes, Your Highness,' I said as I felt my body go stiff.

'Have you used it?'

'Only on one horse and it was too upsetting to him. With all due respect,' I said hesitantly, 'I don't feel it's a good idea.'

The tension in the barn mounted as everyone held their breath waiting for the King to respond.

'I think it's a great idea,' he bellowed. 'This bit will pierce the tongues of our horses in battle. The blood dripping out of their mouths will scare our enemies, causing them to run like mad!' At this, he flipped his head back and roared in laughter and the other men joined in. Then just as quickly, he coldly called out, 'Put it on the white horse and ride him out here!'

I froze, and then panicked. *No, not Magic! Any horse, but not Magic! He trusts me to protect him!* Yet if I crossed the King one more time, I'd lose my position at the stable and never see Magic again. I might even be killed … Perhaps I could let Magic loose before they got to him. They would never catch him and he would return to me when I called for him later. Running and panting, I pushed past rows of other uniformed men to get to my horse.

'Wait!' I called as I turned into his stall only to see the torturous bit I created going into his mouth by another soldier's hands. Putting my trembling hand on his neck, I shrunk back, losing my courage, and instead of pulling him away from the men, I felt myself die inside as I succumbed to a sickening feeling of resignation. I was only one man and I couldn't stop them. 'I'm sorry Magic … Please, forgive me.'

I watched as they led Magic to the large arena where a young man jumped on his back as another pulled the leather strap tight around his mouth. The metal shank cut into Magic's tongue. Rearing up, bright red blood dripped from his mouth and down his white neck and chest. Magic searched the crowd for me to help him, but I hid behind a door, filled with a deep sense of dishonour. There behind the door, in an anguish of emotion I contemplated killing myself.

Then the scene pulled away and I found myself back in my bedroom, sobbing with my hands over my face. Magic called to me, 'Now do you understand why I shook when you rode me today?'

'Yes! Oh, my gosh ... no wonder you acted so wild. You could feel all that pain going from my body into yours?'

'That's it exactly,' he responded. 'I'm so thankful you understand that I wasn't being naughty. I simply desired for you to heal and forgive yourself.'

'Yes, but do you forgive me?' I asked, starting to cry again.

Magic paused and simply said, 'I want you to feel my answer. Then you will understand.'

He invited me to relax again and take three long breaths. 'Expand the energetic space between the breaths and go into this pause,' he warmly said.

'Okay, I'm going into the dark open space. I first learned about this pause after my near-death experience. The angels and ascended masters taught me to look here for any answer.'

'Yes. This is the same place. In a moment you will know about my forgiveness toward you. The complete union of our souls will allow your remaining shame and fear to melt away.'

Continuing to breathe and expand the space between the breaths, the pause grew and I stepped into the dark, universal space in my mind. Walking on a suspended bridge, I saw Magic in the distance. As I met his eyes, he nodded his black-and-white head to acknowledge me. In a flash, purple and white light seared through his body. It became so bright I thought it might hurt my eyes. My heart swelled in love as this penetrating light continued to burst through the expansive darkness surrounding us. The brilliance consumed his body until I could no longer see his horse shape. Rainbow-filled prisms then shot out from him and pierced my heart. My chest heaved with emotion as thick, black lava drained out of my feet. Images flashed across my mind's eye like a movie screen. In scene after scene, my fear, shame and guilt about not protecting him moved past my eyes faster and faster. Then the brilliant light grabbed a hold of these images. Wrapping itself around this darkness, it puffed and blinked and removed all traces of shame and guilt until nothing remained except the purple and white light emanating from Magic. It continued to fill every cell, muscle and bone of my body. My heart was now clear and strong.

Asia and her special horse.

Then softly, his voice echoed around me, 'This is how much I love you.'

The Basics of Animal Communication

Let's get started on the basic steps to hearing guidance from your animals.

At the same time as I learned to walk after my near-fatal car accident, I also learned to talk again with the animals. It's amazing how similar this process was for me. After spending three months in a hospital bed, the time came to start walking. My nurses held me up and asked me to take a step. My muscles, however, had no idea how to begin moving because I couldn't remember or feel how to walk. There was no connection between my mind and body. Nothing. Then one of my nurses asked me to close my eyes and feel as she moved my leg for me. Reaching down she lifted and rotated my leg and hip like I was taking a step. It worked! I remembered and started off with a little shuffle. With time, practice and trust, I remembered how to walk. Animal communication works the same way. Once you remember how to use your soul's language, you will start with a shuffle and progress to larger and larger steps until you're clearly communicating with your animals. So, shuffling is good.

Just as your mind telling your muscles to move requires a conversation between your mind and body, talking to animals encompasses a two-way conversation. It requires desire, focus, energy, visualisation, relaxation, breath, pausing and going between the breaths, trust, asking for help, looking to where you are going, feeling all your body parts, shuffling, appreciating and being willing to start again until you are walking and talking at the same time.

Let us start with the basics of how communication can enter into your conscious mind. Then we will move to a meditation to get you feeling the process in your psychophysical system.

The Four Main Paths to Communicating with Animals

Feeling emotions, seeing, hearing and sensing physical awareness are the main pathways you will use to receive telepathic communication from animals.

◄ *Feelings*

Clairsentience, or 'clear feelings', means that you are able to connect with the emotions your animals are sending you, and they are felt in your heart. Start by visualising a wide cone in front of your heart to assist in opening and 'catching' emotions sent from your animals.

◄ *Seeing*

Clairvoyance, or 'clear seeing', means that pictures and images appear like a still photograph or a running film in your mind's eye. The image can happen in a flash or it might stay there until you acknowledge that you see it. To send a picture, visualise in your mind what you want and imagine it floating over to your animal.

◄ *Hearing*

Clairaudience, or 'clear hearing', means that thoughts and words come into your mind from your animal. When sending words to your animal, focus on only one thought at a time.

⁌ *Physical*

You might feel a sensation or wave of physical discomfort somewhere in your body. Maybe your throat will tighten or you will feel a sudden headache. This is the physical pain your animal is experiencing. Check in with yourself to see if you are having the same issue. With practice you will be able to distinguish your own pain from your animal's pain.

Who's Talking?

The number one question I am asked from my students is: 'How do I know if it is the animal sending the message and not just my mind making it up?'

Here are three ways to know if the message is coming from your animal: the speed the communication takes; the tone of the voice; and the arrangement or choice of the words they use.

⁌ *Speed*

The answer will come almost instantaneously. When I formulate a question and start to ask my animal for guidance, before I can finish my sentence the answer is typically already there.

⁌ *Tone*

The animal's voice in your head sounds different than your own voice. It may have an accent from a different country or a higher or lower tone than you speak with.

⁌ *Arrangement*

Animals can speak in a myriad of ways, from child-like to angelic master. However, the one thing you will find yourself thinking over and over again is, 'I never would have said it like that,' or 'I never use those words.'

Your Soul's First Language

Now it is time to get connected with your animal companions and step into the expansive remembering of telepathic connection. This is your soul's first language. Allow your soul to speak to you and feel this healing experience of connection for yourself. Envision a ray of light in your heart and send it out to your animal companion. Once the connection is made, it becomes a joyous union. Even though you 'visualise' this light connection, know that when you feel it, it is very real.

Lastly, when you are asking a question, break it down into small pieces. If you start with, 'What areas of my life need help?' it is too big of a question and you might just hear, 'All of them!' Start by making a list of yes/no questions that are light in nature like 'Do you love to play with me?' Generally, a 'yes' feels like a happy sensation in your heart and a 'no' feels heavy. Try it out! With practice you'll discover your own precise sensations for 'yes' and 'no' answers. Once this method is mastered, you can ask more complex questions but still narrow them down into subjects like health, home, relationships or past lives.

Telepathic communication enables you to connect with animals in your own home as well as around the world. So, if you don't have an animal in your life, it doesn't mean you can't benefit from their insight. Animals such as dolphins, whales and wild mustangs are available to communicate with you. This communication energy has no limits and this includes animals that have passed.

Now find a quiet place with little or no distractions during a time you know your animal is receptive, that is, exercised, fed and relaxed. A prayer is a great way to open up your heart for listening. This is one I like to use:

> *'I call upon the beings of light, with an interest in me and my highest good, and an interest in (animal's name) and their highest good, to join us. I am a clear and perfect channel.'*

Read this short meditation first and then telepathically connect with your animal. Start by gazing softly at your companion or closing your eyes. Ask them this: 'Are you ready to communicate with me? Do you have a message for me in one area of my life?' See, feel or sense a 'yes' or a 'no'. Ask your animal to send you a word, picture or feeling concerning their message. Relax and breathe slowly, visualising your heart and mind opening. See and feel the energetic field around your body growing and expanding. Allow their message to flow to you. What are you hearing? Is there a picture? Is there a sensation in your heart? What are you feeling in your body? Relax into the space or pause between each of your breaths. This will lead you to the pathway of the Divine realm where you can begin your communication with your animal. After sharing conversation, you will both experience a deeper relationship, greater healing and your lives will flourish.

Now, you too can feel, see and hear the wisdom of your animals. You are entering a new frontier where you hold these intuitive and healing conversations with your animals. Your life will be opened in ways you both had imagined and hoped for.

My chestnut-coloured horse, Cajun shares this:

> *'You will never be alone. The spirit and essence of your animals are always with you. Reach out to them and claim your ability to unite intuitively. You are there to assist each other in healing and knowing your soul's light together.'*

Suggestions to Help You Live Extraordinarily by Allowing the Love of Your Animals to Heal You

 Practice hearing words from your animals in your inner intuitive ear.

Start by imagining what they might be saying and let the words flow. Eventually you will hear their direct messages.

Notice how your animals are acting around you.

Notice if your dog, cat or horse stares at you or acts up for no apparent reason. They may have a personal healing message for you. Take a deep breath, open your heart and step into the pause between each breath where the messages of your animal companions reside.

 Create quiet time for you and your animal companions

Put aside five minutes at the same time each day where you say to your companions, 'I am available to hear your messages of healing.' Listen quietly for their guidance and insights.

'Waking up means tearing ourselves away from the mind-numbing distractions we've surrounded ourselves with ... It means standing up and grabbing onto our Lives with both hands and refusing to let go until we've turned them into something we utterly love ...'

Leila Khani

Leila Khani is a freelance writer and a future best-selling author. She is also a world traveller, an avid reader, an animal lover and a life-long learner. She considers herself a gypsy, free and in love with this great, big, awesome adventure called 'Life'. She is currently studying to obtain her PhD in holistic living, which aligns perfectly with her beliefs in whole, balanced lifestyles and authentic living. Her previous schooling is in medicine: she has degrees in biomedicine, medical radiation science and nuclear medicine. However, she had a falling out with Western medicine when she decided she didn't want to be a part of the current 'sickness-care' system. So, she left those pieces of paper behind, dropped the extraneous alphabet soup from her name and is now working on creating her own dream job and dream life according to her standards. And she believes every single person has the privilege of doing the same.

Leila believes we are here but once (that we remember, anyway!) and that we absolutely can make this life as wild and precious as we choose. She currently lives in beautiful northern Ontario, Canada, amid magical lakes and forests. But she considers the whole, wide, wonderful world her Home.

An Extraordinary Journey

LEILA KHANI

Well, hello there, beautiful one. I've been expecting you, and I'm so glad we finally get to meet here and spend some time together. Listen, I know why you've come. I know you've been having some doubts, feeling uncertain and a little lost, wondering if this is all there is to this thing called 'Life'. And the first thing I want to tell you is, 'Don't worry. We've all been there.' I have … and still am sometimes. I know something else, though, with one hundred per cent certainty and zero per cent doubt. And that is that you, me and everyone else are free to create and design the exact kind of perfect Life that we choose. We all have the privilege of crafting our dream jobs, dream relationships and dream lives according to our own standards and no one else's. We absolutely *can* make it as wild and precious as we choose. And that's how we start banishing doubt and fear and uncertainty — by believing in ourselves and in the glorious lives we're creating.

I know you and I are going to be great friends, so I'll tell you something about me. If you had met me just four or five years ago, you would've seen a very different person. Oh, I don't look that different on the outside (I actually look younger now!). But I've changed in ways few people could imagine. I know who I am now, more than ever, and that makes all the difference. My eyes dance now. I dance now … just because. I float along like there's nothing weighing me down … because there isn't. I'm free.

Getting rid of the whole extraneous alphabet soup that was hanging onto my name like a heavy anchor helped a lot (really, between you and me, it looked something like B.Sc.(Hon), BMRS, MRT(N), with a PhD about to attach itself!). Anyway, that's not who I am, so I dropped it. (I'll tell you a little bit more about that later.) The point is that I woke up one day with a thrill of terror and thought: *This can't be my Life. It is SO wrong.* And I wanted to, *needed to,* do something about it. So I have, and I am. I'm working on figuring out my own way, knowing that, darling, there *is* more … so, so much more. And you deserve a Life, also, that's full to bursting with excitement and passion and purpose and meaning. As do we all.

Now, since I'm a self-styled holistic gypsy, we're going to do this in a spirit of fun, if that's okay with you. All through school – grade, high, university and graduate – I had to write a lot of rigid, technical, mundane stuff. Thankfully and happily, I don't have to do that anymore. So, let's you and me lay back, grab something to drink – and maybe some chocolate – and let's get comfy. I have some fuzzy slippers here for you.

I'm a huge fan of adventures – great adventures and small adventures, whether they occur in the vast world outside ourselves or in the even more vast universe within. Whether they involve discovering a new facet to something we love, or discovering a whole new continent, I believe that Life is an adventure (have you noticed?) – the grandest, greatest, most wondrous of them all. Really, when it comes down to it, it is the *only* adventure. And, like I mentioned before, it's up to us to make it extraordinary.

In fact, in the spirit of living extraordinarily, I was just about to take a journey through this greatest of all great adventures called Life. And you chose to drop by at the perfect time because I'd love it if you'd come with me. Just you and me. Right now. Ready? Here we go …

A Story

It's 2006, and I'm depressed. I've never been depressed before … it's the first (and only) time, and I don't even know if that's what you call it. I don't know about trying to diagnose myself, and I don't know about symptoms, which is ironic because I'm in medicine. But, hey! I don't even know to look for symptoms. I mean, come on, I'm the eternally optimistic one! All I know right now is that I hate getting up in the morning. It takes everything out of me, and I don't even know how I do it. Then when I get home, I go straight to my room, which is always dark, and I sleep. I know that I love to sleep. Sometimes I get up to eat something, sometimes I don't. There's a skylight above my bed, and I keep my window open when it rains so I can feel the mist on my face and can see the stars. I can hear the trains outside, too, coming in to be loaded or unloaded; I don't know which. There's some kind of factory back there, hidden by trees, like our big, beautiful house is just a façade for something steel-edged and raw that moves behind it in the dark. And this is what my life will be like for about a year.

Oh, I have incredible friends around me whom I love: we go to the movies and go shopping and throw some really phenomenal parties. But mostly we complain about how much life sucks since we've started clinical placement. We're all medical students, and we spend our days in hospitals, training to be the next generation of scrub-wearing staff. You'd think it'd be prestigious, wouldn't you? Like all those hospital shows on TV. In the midst of all that 'prestige', I write the following entries in my diary:

January 15

I'm awake and it's so early and so dark that I can see nothing but the blinding white of this computer screen. The surrounding blackness seems even blacker because of its glare. I feel so hollow. So sad and depressed and dejected and alone. It feels like all the weight that I've never allowed to touch me is settling in around my head and my shoulders and slowly starting to crush me. I feel like an insect, gathered callously for some outer sign of brilliance, stuck through with pins, impaled and motionless, sealed under glass where I'm struggling and suffocating. The more you move the tighter it gets. I don't want to be this way right now. I don't want to be here. And, of course, I don't know what it is that I want, so how can I change?

July 3

My heart is aching. It feels like a cannon ball sitting in my chest, dull and grey, heavy with worry and regret and fears. I am so 'blah' at the moment ... sitting here, in this disastrous mess of a room, wasting away more precious seconds of my life. Can you believe

how much time we waste in doing nothing? It appals
me. But I'm so tired all the time. I'm struggling to
deal with working in a monstrous, pastel-scrub-green
hospital, surrounded by monstrous, pastel-scrub-green-
wearing people. It's killing me. It's slowly sucking
the life out of me, leaching away at my soul ...

Thus was the beginning of my whole being telling me that the Western medical health-care system was not for me. Move to the future and now I can say that, yes, I have my own very clear opinions about that system. I do believe it's fundamentally a sickness-care system that treats people like symptoms and drugs them to death. I know that some of it is useful and has its place, but I believe in a more holistic, integral, preventative kind of system, and I'm glad to see us beginning to move in that direction. I'm actually studying right now to obtain a PhD in holistic living, which is much more in alignment with my beliefs in whole, balanced lifestyles and authentic living.

My experience is my own and I would never force my opinion on anyone. I just wanted to illustrate through my story that I was clearly in the wrong field as far as my Life's work was concerned.

So ... why did I do it then? That's what you're thinking, isn't it? Why go to school for eight years – yes, eight! – to study something I loathed? It's okay; I get it all the time. And truly, it wasn't the studying I loathed. I always loved school. I love learning, still, and will do it, hopefully, every day for the rest of my Life. It was just that final clinical placement year that tore out my heart and snuffed the light from my eyes. And do you know why I was there? It's the same reason most people drag themselves out of bed in the morning to suffer through jobs they despise. It's all about the Expectations (with a capital E). From parents, family, friends, kids, society. 'Them'. You know Them. That mythical entity you think you have to impress, who makes you believe It has all the answers and makes all the rules; who somehow, from around the time you start walking and talking, lets you know that you have to grow up, get real, study hard, work hard, struggle, suffer, sacrifice and keep putting off your Life until you're ready to retire, a.k.a die, by which time you have no life left to live.

I wish I had known who the hell They were so I could have told Them to 'eff off'. And They'd have probably keeled over because coming from me it would have been blasphemy. After all, I was the star student, the good girl, the prodigy, the Governor-General-award-winning-scholar, the brightest and best around. I was *supposed to* become a doctor, or land some other high-paying, glamorous-sounding, envy-inspiring, time-stealing job. So, I can't tell you what a stir I caused when I refused to write my board exams. Woweee! The mass confusion and disappointment were resounding and palpable. They still are. Oh, I finished that year and completed all the necessary schooling. But I skipped the exams, thereby rendering myself uncertified and guaranteeing I couldn't be hired in that field (and I won't be!).

Why? Because I just knew. I knew I couldn't spend the rest of my Life doing that kind of work ... and not because it's intrinsically 'bad' or 'wrong' (nothing is), but because it's bad and wrong *for me.* And *spending* my Life is exactly what I would've been doing: tossing away my precious hours and days like bright pennies down a dull drain. I couldn't. So, for the first time in my life, I veered away from the expected and turned down a different road. My own.

For the first time in my life, I veered away from the expected and turned down a different road. My own.

It hasn't been, and still isn't, easy. My road has bumps in it. Sometimes there's a fog covering it that's so thick I can't see where I'm going, and I don't know what the hell I'm doing here. I need to stop a lot, take breaks, walk around and breathe. But I keep going ... because this road is mine, and it's the most beautiful place I've ever seen. Besides, that *other* road I was on was heading to no place good: I'm pretty sure it runs right off a cliff. Dead end.

But this, happily, is *not* the end! This was a story ... my story, yes, but it's only one. I have many, many others, and still none of them make me all of who I am. Just like you, my brave and beautiful, adventuresome friend. I would love to hear your stories. And when I do, I will never take them to be the sum of all that you are. Plus, stories can be changed and re-defined, even re-written if necessary. That's part of the magic. We can choose what to remember and focus on the beauty, all the good we've experienced, all the love we've shared and forget the rest. I think we need to acknowledge that stories are useful if we can use them to learn and heal and grow. But we have to be careful about letting them define us. The past is not who we are. We need to make our peace with it, use only what serves us and let the rest go.

Hey, I'm totally grateful for this story! I'm glad I got to live it: in the big city, in my own apartment, facing something that scared me. I'm glad I met my friends, who are some of the best I have still. I'm glad I got to share a huge house with some of them where we had great times that are still talked about and reminisced over! I'm glad I got to share the lives of every single one of my patients. And I'm glad I'm here now, in a better place, able to talk about it with compassion and humour and a huge amount of love. I'm glad I get to use one of the worst times of my Life as a catalyst to propel me into this – the beginning of what is sure to be the best time of my Life so far! Where would I be without it?

This is where it has brought me: travelling along the scary, exhilarating, perfect, pot-holed road of my very own glorious Life – designed by, and destined for, no one else but me. And I can't imagine any other way to go, any other way to be. A little later on, we'll come back here and we'll take a look at what's going on right now. But first I want us to go somewhere else. Okay? Let's go ...

A Dream

It's 2016, and I'm in heaven. No, not literally! I can't die now, Life's too good! It's almost unfathomable that ten short years ago, I was holed up in that dark room, surrounded by a dark cloud, not knowing. Really, just not knowing ... anything ... where to go, what to do, who I was. I want to take that sweet, young me (okay, younger me!) and scoop her up and hold her tight and say, 'Oh, my sweet darling. Don't you worry about a thing! Wait 'til you see what's coming up! It's going to be SO good! Sleep now if you must because you're not going to want to miss this! Save your strength! Here come your wildest dreams!'

Because they have come.

We've just returned from a month in Ireland. The first time, I went for two months and was alone, then I wanted to bring my love there and show him this place that feels like home to me. We travel often, but there are only a few places that speak to you as though you've always known them. They're inside you before you even set foot there. Ireland is like that for me. So are a few other magical islands. Tahiti, Fiji and Polynesia. Greece. Some of the remoter Hawaiians. The next place on our agenda is Egypt ... it's been on my travel list since I was young, and I'm finally going to climb to the top of the Great Pyramid and look out over the world. But, for now, we're home.

There is no darkness in this house. It is as light-filled as green leaves in summer. There is colour in every room. The windows are always open and sheer, white curtains float in homage to the breeze from the sea. I can hear the waves rush up and down the shore, day and night, like a song or the breath in my lungs. Palm trees rustle and the air tastes like flowers. These days, I can't wait to get up in the mornings. I almost jump out of bed and my first thought, every day, is, *Oh my God! I am SO glad to be alive!* Outside, the horses nicker, toss their glorious heads and begin to run through the patchwork of fields, for no other reason than the exhilaration of being alive. The sun slides along the length of their silky blackness and streams out from their billowed tails. Our German Shepherd likes to run alongside the fence with them until she gets tired of the game and comes to lay panting by our side, mine and my love's as we sit together. We are usually on the porch swing, drinking tea with the morning sun, or on the beach with our feet in the sand, watching the sky blaze itself to sleep.

This is where I write and live. This is my Life because I designed it this way. Not only am I wildly successful at what I do, but I write every day because it's what I Love. Articles, blog posts, stories, novels. Whatever it is that's in me to write. Children's books are fun and one of my favourite things to create. My niece helps me with those when she comes to visit, which is pretty often. When you live in paradise, you get a lot of visitors! Remember the ones I told you about before? The disappointed and confused ones? They come, too, and aren't so disappointed anymore; though I think I still confuse them. Maybe they don't know how I do it: manage to live by the sea and 'have it all', needing nothing but a laptop and the magical world of my own thoughts. Maybe they don't know they can have it all, too ... but they can, and so can you.

This is one of my dreams, the big-picture version, but I have many others. And I have no doubt at all that it's real, and that the 'me' writing on the beach surrounded by love and sea-breeze and animals is just waiting patiently for this present 'me' to show up. That's how I think it works. I think it's all there already, and we just need to move into it by changing our thoughts and beliefs and actions, becoming that person and aligning ourselves with our dreams.

Leila 'having it all'.

So, I'd like to ask you, my fellow wild and free soul, to articulate what your dreams are. Write them down. The huge, daunting, world-altering dreams you're afraid to mention and the small, precious, ordinary dreams you've held onto all along. They will become your Life if you let them ... because, guess what? I've always known I was a writer. When I was two years old, as soon as I could grasp a crayon, I was writing and drawing and making up stories on coloured construction paper. And then, somewhere along the way, someone (Them again!) made me believe that writing and drawing were only pastimes that I couldn't make a real living from. I was too smart, anyway; I had to get a 'real' job. Well. I'm pleased to announce that I've got one. It's called Living the Wildest, Freest, Best Freakin' Life I Possibly Can. And it's as real as it gets.

Phew! We're doing a lot of adventuring today aren't we, dear friend? We've just visited a story and a dream, and we could keep doing that forever. But we won't. I wanted to take you to the past and the future to show you that those are nice places to visit if you use them constructively. But you can't live there. Some people do. They get so caught up in regrets about the past or worries about the future they end up missing out on the only place that's really *real*. Let's not do that. Let's go back, you and me, to that road we were on a little while ago, and I'll tell you everything you want to know about learning how to really *live* …

A Reality Check

It's 2011. Right here, right now. I'm sitting on the couch in my boyfriend's apartment, in my favourite T-shirt and black capris, feeling slightly too warm and wanting to go stand outside in the rain I can hear pelting down on the other side of the window. The sky out there is a uniform sheet of white. The clock's ticking a little too loudly, though I can only hear it if I focus on it, and I'm starting to get hungry. I keep distracting myself with thoughts of food, wanting to shower and wanting my boyfriend to pop in from work unexpectedly so I can kiss him. I am writing this, one of my first real writing assignments ever, and I'm excited and terrified and tense and so, SO ecstatically happy. This is where I am, today, in this moment, on my great, winding road in the midst of my great, winding adventure of a Life. Where are you? Right now? See it, seize it and love it. Because it's all you've got. This is where Living happens. It is clear … and real … and perfect … and all your fancy stories and all your lofty dreams couldn't even exist without it. It is a 'present' in more ways than one.

And you've come here, right now, to sit with me on this couch and talk with me about living an extraordinary Life. First things first: I'm not an expert … at least, not for you. The only expert who knows about how to live your precious Life is You. I am, however, an expert for myself and I can tell you what I think and believe and know to be true for me. And through our sharing, perhaps we can kindle the lights within each other and go forth more ablaze than we were before. I want to help you shine.

The only expert who knows about how to live your precious Life is You.

So … how do you Live Extraordinarily? Right now?

The first step I know is: Wake up. For the love of all the gods and goddesses ever revered, the world needs us awake. It needs us to dash the mist from our eyes and really see what's been in front of us all along. We can't keep moving through our lives and the world in an unconscious stupor. We can't keep ignoring the stirrings, the pull, the voice, saying, 'There IS more than this! Don't settle! Look!' Waking up means tearing ourselves away from the mind-numbing distractions we've surrounded ourselves with. It means taking a good, long, clear-eyed look at ourselves and at the situation of our Lives. It means questioning, growing, acting and changing what needs to be changed. It means standing up and grabbing onto our Lives with both hands and refusing to let go until we've turned them into something we utterly love and can't live without.

Waking up is scary, especially waking up one day to discover we're in a whole new world. Sometimes we'll feel alone and misunderstood. Sometimes we'll feel a lack of direction, like we don't know what to do, where to go, or to whom we belong. We'll feel like we're the only ones 'like us' that we know and that we sometimes need to hide our true selves in order to keep fitting in, feeling accepted and appearing 'normal'. We'll put up façades and try to pretend we're still asleep ... until we can't.

I know about the fears. About being afraid of leaving others behind, or of being alienated. Afraid of stepping up, of stepping out ... of being criticised and judged ... and of shining too brightly. But I know this too: My greatest fear of all is of living small and stifled forever. And despite all the fears, my longing for *more* is greater and stronger. There is a yearning. A dreaming. Wishing and hoping. There is a *knowing* in me, deeper and more immutable than all the rest. What keeps me awake most of all is my not wanting to go back to sleep. Stay awake with me.

Since you've come this far with me and are still here, I think you already know this. And since your eyes are wide open and you're willing to see, you can now start investigating for yourself. This is the fun part! So answer me this: What do YOU want? Regardless of what everyone else thinks and wants for you. You might not know yet, and that's okay. But after waking up and learning to listen to yourself, to what you need and love, is the next step, and is just as important.

Here's somewhere you can start: Whatever negative kind of feelings you have with regard to other people, be they guilt, fear, shame, debt … get rid of them. Ignore them. Tell them to shut the hell up if you have to (the feelings, not the people, though sometimes that's necessary too!). Because you know what? You didn't come here for Them. You didn't come here for anyone but yourself, and you came here to be happy. The bottom line is that you don't owe anyone anything … just you. Let them call you selfish or whatever else they want to say. What others think of you doesn't matter and has more to do with them than it ever does with you. They'll think what they want no matter what, anyway. I've also realised that as I learn to let go of judging other people (which is still a work in progress, I assure you!), I find other people's judgments of me matter less and less. It's totally freeing. But … let's get back to you and finding out what you want your Extraordinary Life to look like.

If there's somewhere you can go, as far away as possible from everyone you know, where you can be totally alone for a little while, do it! And ask yourself questions like: What do I love? Truly love …. so much that it burns like a flame in my heart? What did I used to love when I was younger? What makes me smile and laugh and feel like crying with joy? Where would I love to go or to live? What do I value above anything else? What's precious to me? What will I regret … at the end … if I don't do it? Or see it? Or say it? And then, my darling, get on with it!

Whatever makes you close your eyes, throw your head back and run, shiver, scream with the ecstasy of being alive …. Do that. Life is so short … so absurdly short. Don't you see what that means? You can't waste it. Everyone thinks it'll last forever. It won't. It will pass by in a blink. The days, months, years, will fly by and we'll be left wondering where they went, regretting. But that shouldn't make you sad, or depressed (I'm not going there again!). It should make you want to squeeze the life and love and joy out of every single moment. Let's do it right now! Here's a game we can play. I'm sure you've heard of it before, but I want you to really do it. I will, too.

It's called 'Four Weeks', and that's how long you have left to live. Just four more weeks on this gorgeous, blue-green globe. What do you do? Do you say, 'Well, I think I'll regret not being able to work a few more hours, or veg in front of the TV a little more?' Eff no! Or, if so, that's your prerogative and I won't judge you. But if I had four weeks left, this is what I'd do:

I would find some reason, any reason, to laugh every day. I'd get on the phone and call everyone I love just to tell them so. I'd get in my car and go visit my family and friends, irrespective of distance and gas prices, to hug them, and to laugh and cry with them. I'd spend a whole day, at least, with my sister, sitting with her and telling her how gorgeous she is. I would dance more and sing more. I'd eat popsicles and ice cream galore. I would write my heart out. I'd give all of my stuff away. I would ride a Friesian horse and see another sunrise and sunset. I'd find a way to stand on the cliffs of Moher in Ireland again, to climb the Great Pyramid, run along the Great Wall and swim the Great Barrier Reef. I would forgive everyone everything, especially myself. I would love them all exactly as they are. I'd go float in the lake at home and refuse to take a single moment for granted. I'd make love, with my love, as much as humanly possible and I'd kiss him in that breathless way of ours until I had no breath left in me.

Oh, God, there's more. There will always be more. And just writing about it, I feel the urge to get out and start doing as much as I can ... which is the point. So, write your list. And here's a secret: There's no such thing as death, not really. But it serves its purpose in getting you to really live.

So go. Do. Laugh. Cry. Fall. Fly. Dare. Try. Love. Be. Live ... just live. As authentically as you possibly can. As boldly and brightly, or as simply and quietly as you want. Explode like a firework when you're called to, and sleep like a baby when you need to. And get this: There's no such thing as a mistake ... or failure. Those are words They made up to keep you small and scared. There are ways of learning how **not** to do things, but then you just try something new and learn differently.

So, since there's no such thing as failing, and a whole bunch of new things to try ... as you're reading this, right now, what ideas are you getting? What's beginning to whisper to you? Your soul already knows what it loves. Take classes to learn about things that interest you. Learn a new language. Play an instrument. Do work that you adore. Eat a strawberry. Move and live wherever you want, to those magical places calling you home. Open your mouth and yell if you've been quiet for too long. Get

There's no such thing as death, not really. But it serves its purpose in getting you to really live.

up and go run around the block. Or curl up in your bed and take a nap.

And before you even start having any thoughts along the lines of: 'But who am I to … ?' Stop! I'll tell you who you are. You are unique and precious and perfect. In all the great turnings of time, there has never been, nor ever will there be anyone just like you. The extraordinary, magnificent, beautiful thing that you are will not come this way again. Ever. So there is nothing you need to prove or to accomplish to earn your value. You are already priceless, just because you exist.

And here's a little side note. (I want to mention this to assuage you, just in case … I don't want you to think I'm trying to turn you into some kind of self-absorbed, conceited, uncaring, single-minded narcissist - I know you wouldn't think so). This is the truth: **Unless you're totally full, you have nothing to give to others anyway.** Only when you're happy and fulfilled and passionate and on purpose and in love with your Life, can you have any of it spill over to anyone else. You can't give what you don't have, and that's a fact. Now, let's get back to the truth about You!

You are enough. You are more than enough, of everything. Beautiful enough, young enough, smart enough, good enough, rich enough, brave enough. Even if from this moment on you choose to seclude yourself in a cave (Please don't! We'll miss you!), you have already changed the world. It is already better for your having come. The entire universe has already grown, evolved, and been irrevocably altered and improved because of your existence. Your being here has already changed everything forever – and all that without you even knowing! Imagine what you could do, intentionally or not! Now imagine the wonders and miracles you could perform, being aware of how special and essential and powerful you truly are. There is *nothing* you cannot do. Have you ever heard Them say: 'You can't create something out of nothing'? That's a blatant lie. Of course you can! That's how the world actually works. Everything that now exists was at first just a thought. It is absolutely possible, no, inevitable, to create anything you can imagine or think of or dream.

So dream it. Ask yourself, 'What kind of Life would make me jump out of bed every morning, saying: Man! I am SO glad to be alive?' Then start living it, any way you know how. You'll know you're on the right path … you'll feel it. It feels like happiness … and freedom … and gratitude …

and huge love. For no reason. Create a Life that feels like that as much as possible, and you'll be more than okay. Don't worry, I'll help you. And go wild. Please. I need someone to dream wild dreams with.

So. There we have it for now. I think our journey together is coming to a close. Oh, not for good! Since we've taken this trip together, you and I, we're bonded for life. Adventures never really end, anyway. I can't tell you how glad I am to have had you with me through all this. And I don't know about you, but I've got a traveller's itch now … I'm excited and looking forward to taking another trip sometime very soon. That's what happens to us wild and free birds. Always seeking, exploring, yearning to fly. Remember, it all begins with you, and loving yourself is the most important thing in the world, without which nothing else matters. So if you head out again, don't forget to keep me posted! I want to hear all about your adventures from now on. Truly.

Suggestions to Help You Live Extraordinarily by Being Fully Present and Living in the NOW

 ## *Get some perspective*

Right now, there are over 6 billion people living on this planet. In all of Earth's recorded history, there have been billions more. **Go outside tonight and really look at the stars.** There are billions of those, too. If you're in a city, get out of it for a while and look up, or study an astronomy book or class. Imagine those billions of other galaxies with their billions of other planets, all with their own special Life forms. Now, in all this mind-boggling vastness of possible beings, there is only one YOU. Just one. Now. And for all time. Do you see, then, how precious you are? Never take yourself or your Life for granted. Think of this often … and go look at the stars if you ever start to feel small and insignificant.

Get curious

Start taking great interest in your own Life. Become a detective for your Self. *Make lists:* lists of things you Love; that make you laugh; of places you adore; of the people who mean the most to you; of the things you Love about them; and the things you Love about yourself. Take stock. Record it all and re-visit it often. Your sweet Life is worthy of study. When you know what you Love and what lights you up, you can live from that more often.

 ## Get grounded

Imagination is one of the greatest gifts you possess. But if you want to really live in the 'now', you need to ground yourself deep in your beautiful body. We're here and we're human, after all. So, *slow down.* Really feel what your hands are touching. *Stop and stand and feel the earth under your feet.* Walk slowly and marvel in your body's freedom. Look closely at the sky and the grass and your Love's eyes. *Stretch.* Savour the next thing you eat, as if it's your last. Learn to Love yourself shamelessly.

GET YOUR EXTRAORDINARY
FREE GIFT BONUS

Leila Khani is kindly offering a **FREE BONUS GIFT** to all readers of this book.

21 Ways to Love Yourself Shamelessly

A free eBook to help you live an extraordinary life.

Simply visit the web page below and follow the directions to directly download *21 Ways to Love Yourself Shamelessly.*

www.holisticgypsy.com

Final Thoughts

VANESSA TALBOT

Now that you've explored these keys to living remarkably, I hope that you will continue to apply them to your own life and become expert at The Art of Living a Lusciously Spirited, Vibrant Life!

Of course, we never truly become an expert. We are constantly learning and evolving, and the moment we stop learning is the day we die.

I encourage you, in the spirit of leaping, skipping, stepping, crawling or tippy-toeing into an extraordinary life, whichever may be the right method for you, that you reward yourself with the FREE BONUS Giveaways of the wisdom guides and their keys that most resonated with you. And then use them! You must put into action the guidance that has spoken to you, otherwise your life will not change.

The teachers within this book each honoured you with a personal story of their own life. I know that for some their story was difficult to tell. But with even greater honour to you, they gave you their knowledge and experiences to empower and uplift you to becoming in your own mind – Extraordinary YOU! For indeed, you are already extraordinary. You only must allow YOU to shine.

In this book I introduced you to this simple truth: it's living in appreciation for the little everyday things that make for a BIG life. I'd like you to stop waiting for the larger, more momentous episodes of life, and also the stuff – all the possessions and wants we have to have – to make you feel happy and good. These occasions are infrequent and short-lived, and along with it so will be your happiness. I'd like to remind you to practice every day appreciation for what you do have, while knowing that what you desire is on its way. Get into the habit of noticing, and nurturing, the unspectacular good things that happen to you. The extraordinary rests always within the seemingly un-extraordinary. The little things of every day.

Camile Araujo gently nudged you to tap into your inner wisdom and listen to the voice within. That can take some practice, especially if you are used to listening to your rational mind – your head – rather than to your heart – your inner knowing. And it also enables great Trust, as the ego, otherwise known as our rational mind, always wants to convince us that it is right. It will shout to get your attention; while on the other hand the inner voice is often just a whisper. Learn to listen for, and trust, what your inner knowing is whispering to you.

Maria Russo told you through her story that you can learn to follow your own true path and perhaps come to the realisation of it earlier than she did. The earlier we learn to listen to our own instincts about what is right for us, the more likely we are to be saved from years of internal suffocation from living in a life that is not right. But it is never too late to follow your true Self, no matter what your age.

Cynthia Zeki's heartfelt advice to get out of your left-brain world of rationality and what makes sense and move into the peace and beauty of *Heart Living* would be perfect timing for many. Most of us do live in our analytical left-brain, thinking out our lives. Yet that, in most cases, doesn't make for our best lives. Simply put, Heart Living is living in balance between the thinking left-brain and the creating, imaginative right-brain. As Cynthia states, 'Heart Living understands that your own truth, the very centre of who you are and what is right for you, is neither a thought nor an idea but a feeling.'

Fear is the biggest killer of dreams. It resides over most as an invisible, smothering fog that slowly snuffs out the hope inside. **Cath Edwards** encourages you to know that Fear will always be around. It is how you personally see that surrounding fog that reflects the state of your life. Is it something impenetrable to run away from; to escape to where you don't have to face fear anymore? ... And if you do, do you find that the place you have escaped to is the even more frightening cave of regret? Cath clearly showed us that the fog of fear is something to push on through, knowing full well that once you begin to rise above the mist, the road first becomes visible then crystal clear. And then nothing ... absolutely nothing ... is scary anymore. In other words, *feel the apprehension and do it anyway!*

Change your beliefs; change your life. **Sue Crosbie** had a belief she would walk again no matter what the doctors said. And so she did! Beliefs are stored in your mind, captured from your experiences or inherited from others. Some beliefs are important for our survival; some support us and our aspirations favorably, while some, rather many, don't. If you have underlying beliefs that are holding you back from living the life you want, there are methods as Sue suggests that will help you change those beliefs to something else that will empower rather than hinder. Methods such as coaching and NLP, but it can also be as simple as the daily practice of meditation. Explore what is helpful to you.

Ah! The world of men and women and 'The Balance'. Women all too often avoid the male dominated world of business, believing that they don't have the ability to do many of those top management and business positions. **Bianca Carroll** revealed a surprising little secret; that even though we are supposedly in this new world of equal opportunity and equality, for many women their own minds have yet to catch up with the idea. For many of us, we are still getting stuck with the menial office duties at work, and at home it's the housework, cooking the meals and getting the children ready for school. But is it by choice because the female heart will forever lie at home in nurturing and caring, or is it because we don't yet believe we can have more ... if we want it? It's an interesting question, and one to ask of yourself. The choice, of course, all comes down to you and what you want for your own life.

A healthy body often reflects a healthy mind and life. **Minda Lennon** gave you the tips, and science, to living in extraordinary wellness – in both body and mind, for each is a reflection of the other. Live with mindfulness about what you put in your body, for though it is indeed just a container for the 'real you' that resides within, it is your internal spirit's temple while you are here on earth – and it too needs nourishing so it can do the job it was meant to do. So treat it with the respect, dignity and love fit for the loving house it is.

Relationship Coach **Ghania Dib** impressed that it is just as important to be there for *Yourself* as it is to be there for your partner. This is a crucial part of creating healthy relationships and ultimately living a happy live.

Self-care, putting your needs right up there with those of your partner and children, is an essential component of any partnership and family situation. Yet for women this is too often neglected and missed.

The healing power of connecting with animals is widely known, yet so many still see animals as a possession, a commodity, or worse, as something lower than the human race. Fit to use and abuse. While the truth is animals are special, intelligent and emotional beings in their own right, just as we are. Animal communicator **Asia Voight** showed how creating bonds with animals, whether they be a pet or a wild creature, can heal broken hearts and souls, give hope where there was none, and, most importantly, provide companionship, purpose and love. Right now, your own pets and animals may hold a special key for your life.

And lastly, I hope you were as uplifted by **Leila Khani**'s delightful journey as I was. From always being the good girl and suffering the burden and consequences of trying to live up to others' expectations and wishes for her, to now dancing through life on a pathway that nobody picked for her … except herself. May you be delivered with the same joy as she as you skip along your own sparkling path.

All of the wonderful insights and tools shared by our authors are not the only keys to an extraordinary life. There are limitless ways and opportunities for you to truly live life to the immense measures of greatness, pleasure, exhilaration, fulfillment and satisfaction that by the very act of being born you deserve.

I think there is only one distinct point to remember about how to be Extraordinary and how to Live Extraordinarily, and that is this:

The answer to 'How' is 'Yes'.

You need to say 'Yes' more than you do 'No'. You need say one simple but committed YES to Life.

'Yes' to the How's we've given you here, and 'Yes' to the many more How's that are yet to come to you. Such a simple art – the willingness to say 'Yes'. But herein lies the Art to living a Spirited, Luscious, Vibrant, and Extraordinary Life. Allow your heart and soul to say **YES** far more than just your lips, and the art of living extraordinarily will take care of itself.

Acknowledgments

Time for Thank You's

As the compiler of this book, it is my name that is given the largest credit on the cover. I find that a little awkward for there are far more than just me who have been involved with putting this book together.

My story is only a small portion of this book. There are ten other amazing women who have offered as inspiration their stories and what life lessons they've learnt. To each one of them, I thank you for your courage in putting your life out there for all to read and for the wisdom you share. And most of all, for joining me on this journey in getting **Extraordinary YOU** out there in the hope that we may inspire others to look beyond their current realities and build more for their life if they desire. So, to the other authors of this book: *Cath Edwards, Sue Crosbie, Camile Araujo, Maria Russo, Cynthia Zeki, Leila Khani, Minda Lennon, Ghania Dib, Asia Voight* and *Bianca Carroll,* thanks for travelling with me. I hope it's been a great trip so far!

Of all these wonderful writers, I'd like to give a special mention to *Camile Araujo* for the enthusiasm and gusto with which she's approached this book.

I was lucky to find our copyeditor, *Wendy Millgate* of *Wendy & Words,* who worked on this project with patience and diligence. With eleven completely different voices to work with, she went beyond the call of duty on many occasions. Though Wendy jokingly refers to herself as 'Picky Pete', I am grateful for her professionalism along with her easygoing nature, particularly when as a whole we authors stretched her reasoning processes quite a bit at times.

Finally, my gratitude to *Kylee* at *The Publishing Queen.* Kylee knows the publishing industry inside out, helping me tremendously with the whole process of getting the **Extraordinary YOU** published and into readers' hands.

In all, a wonderful team effort. **Thanks to all!**

About Vanessa Talbot

A self-professed country girl living in regional New South Wales, Vanessa views herself as an ordinary woman ... living an extraordinary life. With her first foray into business, together with her husband Vanessa built the business from zero to a multi-million dollar company within two years – while working only three afternoons a week! Though financially rewarding, she found the industry she was in emotionless and uninspiring, and after facing the difficult question, 'What if my whole life has been wrong?' this naturally shy scaredy cat took a leap into the unknown. A leap to rediscover her Real Self.

On this new pathway of allowing passion to intoxicate her life, she uncovered an old flame – writing – and was seduced by a new love: inspiring others to discover and follow their own paths to a spirited, fulfilling and momentous life.

Now enjoying abundance in all areas of her life – an abundance of Love, Time, Money, Freedom, Fun and Passion – Vanessa is blessed to have as her reality a wonderful life on a country property with the man of her dreams, her beautiful five-year-old daughter, her other 'kids' (four gorgeous ponies), and the wildlife and nature that surrounds them.

A Certified Life and Performance Coach, NLP Practitioner, Matrix Therapist, Author, Presenter, Inspirational Speaker AND, to add extra zing to the credentials, an Australian Wildlife Carer, Vanessa has an extraordinary awareness of what it truly means to be alive. The force behind the Living Extraordinarily movement, Vanessa shares through her daily blog, *The Year of Living Extraordinarily,* the truth about expanding experience and living the life you truly want and desire by sharing the magic of the everyday.

She believes in success on your own terms ... and knows it is within everyone's essence to achieve it with ease. Vanessa teaches this empowering message via her coaching practice, Extraordinary Beings – Personal Success Creation, an inspirational and transformational coaching service designed to empower people to discover their own unique version of success ... and then create and live it! With her Writers Success Creation, she provides a proactive service for guiding and energising Inspirational, Motivational, Self-Help and Spiritual authors to write their book, have it published and build an audience to ensure the book sells.

Vanessa is the author and compiler of *Extraordinary YOU ... The Art of Living a Lusciously Spirited, Vibrant Life* and the forthcoming books, *The Year of Living Extraordinarily* and *365 Ways to Live Extraordinarily,* both to be released in 2012. She successfully coaches and mentors clients across both Australia and the USA in Living Extraordinarily so that their aspirations for Life and Success are no longer dreams but a Reality.

Contributors' Directory

There are eleven amazing voices that have helped to make this book possible. Many of them have their own books and other personal growth products. They welcome you to contact them directly for more information.

CAMILE ARAUJO – THE VOICE WITHIN

Trained Demartini Method™ Facilitator, Author, Inspirational Speaker

Email: camile@camilearaujo.com
Website: www.camilearaujo.com
Facebook: www.facebook.com/camilearaujo.thevoicewithin
Book: Journey Beyond Happyville (Pub. mid-2012)

BIANCA CARROLL – BIANCA CARROLL CONSULTING

Qualified Practicing Insurance Broker, Diploma in Financial Services, Consultant & Trainer of Extended DISC, Business and Performance Coach, Team Coach and Facilitator, Cert IV Life Coaching, Certified Practitioner of Neuro-Linguistic Programming

Address: PO Box 1882, Bathurst, NSW 2795. Australia
Email: info@biancacarrollconsulting.com
Website: www.biancacarrollconsulting.com
Facebook: www.facebook.com/biancacarrollconsultingpage

SUE CROSBIE – SPIRITED WOMEN COACHING

Master Practitioner of NLP and Hypnotherapy, Certified Practitioner Matrix and Timeline Therapies, Bachelor of Economics (SocSc), Cert IV Life Coaching, Cert IV Training and Assessment

Email: sue@timeforyouaudios.com
Website: www.timeforyouaudios.com

CATH EDWARDS – YES YOU CAN COACHING

Transformational Coach and Hypnotist specialising in 'fearless' living. Internationally accredited Life Coach, NLP Practitioner, Transformational Hypnotist, Stress Management Facilitator, Certified Practitioner of Matrix & Timeline Therapies, Consultant & Trainer of Extended DISC, Dip Welfare, Dip Community, Grad Dip Adult Ed & Training, Master of Safety & Marriage/Funeral Celebrant.

Email: cath@yesyoucancoaching.com

Website: www.yesyoucancoaching.com *and* www.womenlovinglife.com

Facebook: www.facebook.com/yesyoucancoaching

GHANIA DIB – PHILOSOPHY - LIVE, LOVE & THRIVE; GHANIA DIB & ASSOCIATES

Freelance Journalist, Lawyer (LLB (Hons)), Bachelor of Commerce (Usyd), Inspirational Speaker, Dip. Life Coaching, NLP Performance Coach, Practitioner of Neuro-Linguistic Programming, Practitioner Matrix Therapist, Accredited Consultant & Trainer of Extended DISC, Human Behaviour Specialist, Certified Mediator

Email: ghania@ghaniadib.com

Website: www.philosophylivelovethrive.com *and* www.ghaniadib.com

Facebook: www.facebook.com/GhaniaDibandAssociates
www.facebook.com/PhilosophyLiveLoveandThrive

Book: A Glimmer of Hope (working title) (Pub. 2012)

LEILA KHANI – HOLISTIC GYPSY

Previous Life: *Biomedical Biologist, Medical Radiation Scientist, Nuclear Medicine Technologist*
Current Life: *Freelance Writer, Author, PhD in Holistic Living*

Email: leilakhani@hotmail.com

Website: www.holisticgypsy.com

Facebook: www.facebook.com/leilakhani.writer

MINDA LENNON – FIGURE 8 WELLNESS

Dip. Life Coaching; NLP Practitioner; NLP Performance Coach; Consultant and Trainer of Extended DISC; Practitioner Matrix Therapies; Trainer of Coaching; Cert. III and IV Fitness; Effective Movement trainer

Email: mlennon@figure8wellness.com.au

Website: www.figure8wellness.com.au
           www.forwomenseekingwellness.blogspot.com/

Facebook: www.facebook.com/Figure.8.Wellness

Book: I am woman - the art of being you (Pub. Nov. 2011)

MARIA RUSSO – THE GROWING SOUL

Author, Inspirational Speaker, Licensed Clinical Social Worker, Psychotherapist

Email: healing@MariaRussoLcsw.com

Website: www.MariaRussoLcsw.com *and* www.TheGrowingSoul.com

Facebook: www.facebook.com/TheGrowingSoul *and*
           www.facebook.com/MariaAngelaRusso

Book: The Growing Soul (Pub. 2012)

VANESSA TALBOT – EXTRAORDINARY BEINGS SUCCESS CREATION; THE YEAR OF LIVING EXTRAORDINARILY

Author, Inspirational Speaker, Dip. Life Coaching, NLP Performance Coach, Certified Practitioner of Neuro-Linguistic Programming, Certified Practitioner Matrix Therapies

Email: vanessa@extraordinarybeings.com

Website: www.extraordinarybeings.com *and*
           www.theyearoflivingextraordinarily.com

Facebook: www.facebook.com/ExtraordinaryBeings *and*
           www.facebook.com/TheYearofLivingExtraordinarily

Book: The Year of Living Extraordinarily (Pub. 2012) *and*
           365 Ways to Live Extraordinarily (Pub. 2012)

ASIA VOIGHT – ASIA VOIGHT PROFESSIONAL ANIMAL COMMUNICATOR

Professional Animal Communicator, Intuitive Counsellor, Teacher, Inspirational Speaker, Author and Facilitator of Dolphin and Whale Trips

Phone: USA 608-438-Asia (2742)

Email: Asia@AsiaVoight.com

Website: www.AsiaVoight.com

Facebook: www.facebook.com/asiavoightanimalcommunicatorandintuitive

Book: Burned Back to Spirit, Awakening Your Intuitive Powers by Way of One Woman's Near Death Experience. (Pub. 2012)

CYNTHIA ZEKI – SPARK OF THE HEART

Author, Inspirational Speaker, Radio Host, Founder, Teacher, and Practitioner of Spark of the Heart Energy Healing

Email: cynthia@sparkoftheheart.com

Website: www.sparkoftheheart.com *and* www.iamhealthyradio.com/wake-up-sunshine.html

Facebook: www.facebook.com/sparkoftheheart
www.facebook.com/cynthia.zeki

Book: Heart Living: A Gentle, Loving Guide to Personal and Spiritual Understanding (Pub. 2012)

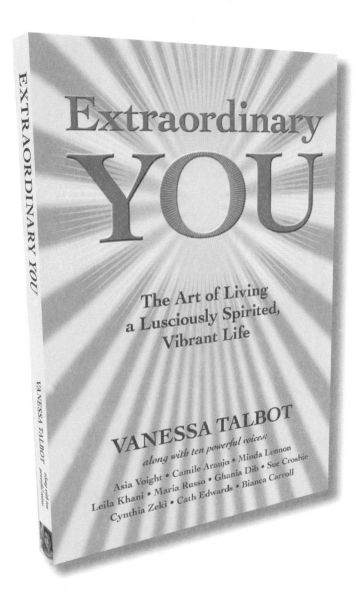